Avadhuta Gita

The Song of the Avadhuta

Translated by

Janki Parikh

Avadhuta Gita Translated by Janki Parikh

ISBN 978-198-10-6148-8

Copyright © 2015 Janki Parikh

All rights reserved. This book or any portion thereof may not be reproduced or used in any manner whatsoever without the express written permission of the publisher except for the use of brief quotations in a book review or scholarly journal.

Publisher contact: info@jankiparikh.com

www.jankiparikh.com

Contents

Introduction	ii
Text and Translation	1
Chapter 1	2
Chapter 2	28
Chapter 3	43
Chapter 4	65
Chapter 5	76
Chapter 6	89
Chapter 7	100
Chapter 8	107

Introduction

The Avadhuta Gita is a majestically lofty masterpiece of an Advaitic Sanskrit song... as ancient as it is lyrically eloquent, as profound as it is elevating, as undeniably compelling as it is sublime!

<u>Advaita Explained</u>

Who or what is God? Would you be surprised to know that in spite of reference to thousands of 'gods' in Hinduism, the highest and final conception of "God" is not a figure with multiple heads and a thousand arms bearing weapons, it is not Brahma-Vishnu-Shiva or their avatars, it is not even a He or a She! God in the highest sense of the term is a formless, genderless, inanimate principle! God is, in fact, the Supreme Universal Principle, or the Ultimate Universal Reality. In other words, God is *Brahman*, also known as the Absolute, the One Universal Consciousness, Supreme Reality, *Sat-Chit-Ananda* (Truth, Consciousness-Bliss). Brahman is the all-pervasive, infinite, unchangeable, indestructible, eternal Reality, the single binding unity behind all the diversity that seems to exist in the universe.

If God is Brahman, then who are you? The other major metaphysical concept in Hinduism is *Atman*, or the Self. Narrowly seen, Atman may be taken to mean the individual soul, but in Hindu Vedanta, Atman is the very foundation, the first principle, the essence of an individual, the *true* Self of an individual beyond identification with phenomena.

Advaita ("*not-two*" in Sanskrit) refers to the recognition that the true Self, Atman, is the same as the highest Reality, or Brahman.

Advaita posits everything there is, is Brahman, and nothing but Brahman. ("Brahmaiva Kevalam Sarvam.") And this Brahman is the same as Atman, or the Self. There is no difference between Brahman and Atman, and no real existence of, or division amongst the myriad characters, objects, emotions, ideas, places and concepts that make up the universe. All these things that seem to exist separately, are in fact, illusions that are spontaneously but very temporarily projected within Brahman. All projections ultimately end, what remains is always Brahman – never-ending, eternal, imperishable, all-pervading, all-knowing, supreme, always pure, always beyond all forms and dualities!

The three principle source texts of Hindu Vedanta – the Upanishads, the Gita and the Brahma Sutras – all present *Advaita* as their central, unifying philosophy in multi-faceted ways. For example, the bold, audacious, supreme spiritual philosophy of Advaita is characterized in several *Mahavakyas*, or the Great Sayings of the Upanishads…

Aham Brahmasmi – *I am Brahman* (Brhadaranyaka Upanishad of the Yajurveda)

Prajnanam Brahma – *Consciousness is Brahman* (Aitareya Upanishad of the Rigveda)

Tat Tvam Asi – *Thou art That* (Chandogya Upanishad of the Samaveda)

Ayam Atma Brahma – *This Atman is Brahman* (Mandukya Upanishad of the Atharvaveda)

So 'ham – *I am That* (Isha Upanishad of the Yajurveda)

The idea of the non-duality of Atman and Brahman is the very fabric and the soul of Vedanta, and it has been expressed in myriad ways for thousands of years!

The Goal of Life and the Process…

According to Vedanta, realization of the absolute oneness of Atman and Brahman through direct, independent, cognitive experience (Anubhuti) is the final goal of all human life, the climax of man's spiritual evolution! This self-realization is what leads to Moksha (liberation), it is what frees mankind from rebirth, karma, misery and every kind of bondage, and leads man to eternal bliss.

How does one achieve independent self-realization?

The thousands of Hindu scriptures that are available talk about very scientific, logical, rational, sequential methods of achieving self-realization. Though not necessarily written by those who have direct experiential awareness, these writings serve the noblest purpose of making Brahman or God available to mankind…

BUT THEN…

There are those writings that flower (I cannot think of any other word but *flower*) straight from the writer's direct experience of the truth, from his own blissful awareness of Advaita or Non-Duality! And how tremendous the difference between these writings and those based on logic and process! What a wonderful taste of bliss these give us! What a glorious, uplifting glimpse into the realms of the writer's exalted state!

The Avadhuta Gita…

The Avadhuta Gita is not only a text flowering from the writer's direct experience – it is the most beautiful, the most profoundly poetic piece of Sanskrit writing I have ever come across! The sheer qualitative height of its Sanskrit vocabulary is matched only by the depth of the ideas it expresses; the final result is eloquent Sanskrit poetry that rolls off the tongue like butter, depositing deep within the reader a powerful series of ideas that are unbelievably rich, lofty, uplifting, freeing, ecstatic, blissful, FINAL!

The Avadhuta Gita is the attempt of an illumined, self-realized sage to describe in words the indescribable experience of the realization of Brahman! His name is Dattatreya, but he calls himself an *Avadhuta* – one who has seen the truth of the Self-as-Brahman, as a consequence of which, the world has fallen away from him. Imagine the state of the one who is alive in this world but free of all its bondage! He lives in bliss and laughs in bliss, with not even a scrap to call his own! He needs nothing from this world, because he is Brahman! He is ever-eternal, unchanging, ever-blissful, abundant, supreme Reality! He is Absolute Universal Consciousness… what can he need from this flimsy, insubstantial world?

I hope you really enjoy immersing yourself into this beautiful song, which is so powerful that even a few lines are enough to give you a taste of the nectar of life lived as Brahman! Read the rest at your own risk – there is no coming back from the Avadhuta's path of freedom and bliss!

Text and Translation

ॐ

Chapter 1

अथ प्रथमोऽध्यायः ।

atha prathama adhyayah |

First Adhyaya

ईश्वरानुग्रहादेव पुंसामद्वैतवासना ।
महद्भयपरित्राणाद्विप्राणामुपजायते ॥ १॥

ishvaranugrahadeva punsam advaita vasana |
mahadbhaya paritranad vipranam upajayate ||1-1||

Indeed, it is by the grace of God that the understanding of non-duality arises in man, and rescues him from the great fear of birth and death!

येनेदं पूरितं सर्वमात्मनैवाअत्मनात्मनि ।
निराकारं कथं वन्दे ह्यभिन्नं शिवमव्ययम् ॥ २॥

yena idam puritam sarvam atmanaiva atmana atmani |
nirakaram katham vande hyabhinnam shivam avyayam ||1-2||

Everything there is, is filled by the Self, and nothing but the Self. How then, do I worship that formless, undivided and limitless Shiva?

पञ्चभूतात्मकं विश्वं मरीचिजलसन्निभम् ।
कस्याप्यहो नमस्कुर्यामहमेको निरञ्जनः ॥ ३॥

panchabhutatmakam vishvam marichijala sannibham |
kasyapyaho namaskuryam aham eko niranjanah ||1-3||

The five elements of which this universe is composed are illusory like water in a mirage. To whom then, shall I bow? I myself am that stainless one!

आत्मैव केवलं सर्वं भेदाभेदो न विद्यते ।
अस्ति नास्ति कथं ब्रूयां विस्मयः प्रतिभाति मे ॥ ४॥

atmaiva kevalam sarvam bhedabhedo na vidyate
asti nasti katham bruyam vismayah pratibhati me ||1-4||

The Self alone is everything, it does not know division or unity. How then, can I say whether it exists or not? I can only gaze at it with wonder!

वेदान्तसारसर्वस्वं ज्ञानं विज्ञानमेव च ।
अहमात्मा निराकारः सर्वव्यापी स्वभावतः ॥ ५॥

vedanta sara sarvasvam jnanam vijnanam eva cha
aham atma nirakarah sarvavyapi svabhavatah ||1-5||

The final essence of all Vedas, all knowledge and all wisdom is only this – "I am the formless Self, all-pervading by my very nature!"

यो वै सर्वात्मको देवो निष्कलो गगनोपमः ।
स्वभावनिर्मलः शुद्धः स एवायं न संशयः ॥ ६॥

yo vai sarvatmako devo niskalo gaganopamah |
svabhavanirmalah shuddah sa evaham na samshayah ||1-6||

That God which comprises everything there is, who is undivided like the sky, who is pure and stainless by nature – no doubt, that is who I am!

अहमेवाव्ययोऽनन्तः शुद्धविज्ञानविग्रहः ।
सुखं दुःखं न जानामि कथं कस्यापि वर्तते ॥ ७॥

aham eva vyayonantah shuddha vijnana vigrahah |
sukham duhkham na janami katham kasyapi vartate ||1-7||

Indeed, I am imperishable and infinite, I am pure knowledge without any division. I do not know joy or sorrow, or how and to whom they appear.

न मानसं कर्म शुभाशुभं मे न कायिकं कर्म शुभाशुभं मे ।
न वाचिकं कर्म शुभाशुभं मे ज्ञानामृतं शुद्धमतीन्द्रियोऽहम् ॥ ८॥

na manasam karma shubhashubham me na kayikam karma shubhashubham me |
na vachikam karma shubhashubham me jnanamritam shuddham atindriyoham ||1-8||

My mind does not have any good or bad karma, my body does not have any good or bad karma, my speech does not have any good or bad karma. I am beyond the senses, the pure nectar of knowledge!

मनो वै गगनाकारं मनो वै सर्वतोमुखम् ।
मनोऽतीतं मनः सर्वं न मनः परमार्थतः ॥ ९॥

mano vai gaganakaram mano vai sarvato mukham |
manatitam manah sarvam na manah paramarthatah ||1-9||

The mind is formless like the sky, and the mind has countless facets. The mind is in the past, the mind is everywhere, yet the mind can never be the supreme truth!

अहमेकमिदं सर्वं व्योमातीतं निरन्तरम् ।
पश्यामि कथमात्मानं प्रत्यक्षं वा तिरोहितम् ॥ १०॥

aham ekam idam sarvam vyomatitam nirantaram |
pashyami katham atmanam pratyaksham va tirohitam ||1-10||

I alone am everything there is, infinite, beyond even space! How then should I perceive my Self? As manifest? As unmanifest?

त्वमेवमेकं हि कथं न बुध्यसे समं हि सर्वेषु विमृष्टमव्ययम् ।
सदोदितोऽसि त्वमखण्डितः प्रभो दिवा च नक्तं च कथं हि मन्यसे ॥ ११॥

tvam evam ekam hi katham na buddhyase samam hi sarveshu vimrishtam avyayam |
sadoditosi tvam akhanditah prabho diva cha naktam cho katham hi manyase ||1-11||

You too are One, how can you not realize that? You are the same imperishable One that is reflected in everyone! You are forever rising like the sun, you are unbreakable, you are supreme! How then, can you believe in either night or day?

आत्मानं सततं विद्धि सर्वत्रैकं निरन्तरम् ।
अहं ध्याता परं ध्येयमखण्डं खण्ड्यते कथम् ॥ १२॥

atmanam satatam viddhi sarvatraikam nirantaram |
aham dhyata param dhyeyam akhandam khandyate katham ||1-12||

Know that the Self is continuous, one, infinite, everywhere. I am the seeker, but I am also the object sought. Where then, is the division in this one unbroken whole?

न जातो न मृतोऽसि त्वं न ते देहः कदाचन ।
सर्वं ब्रह्मेति विख्यातं ब्रवीति बहुधा श्रुतिः ॥ १३॥

na jato no murtosi tvam na te dehah kadachana |
sarvam brahmeti vikhyatam braviti bahudha shrutih ||1-13||

You are neither born nor do you die, nor are you ever the body! It is well-known that "Everything is Brahman." The scriptures have stated this often.

स बाह्याभ्यन्तरोऽसि त्वं शिवः सर्वत्र सर्वदा ।
इतस्ततः कथं भ्रान्तः प्रधावसि पिशाचवत् ॥ १४॥

sa bahyabhyantarosi tvam shivah sarvatra sarvada |
itas tatah katham bhrantah pradhavasi pishachavat ||1-14||

You are that which is both outside and inside, you are Shiva, eternal and all-pervading. Why then, do you run here and there, wandering around like a ghost?

संयोगश्च वियोगश्च वर्तते न च ते न मे ।
न त्वं नाहं जगन्नेदं सर्वमात्मैव केवलम् ॥ १५॥

sanyogash cha viyogash cha vartate na cha te na me |
na tvam naham jagannedam sarvam atmaiva kevalam ||1-15||

There is no union or separation for me or for you. There is no you, no me, no world! There is only the Self everywhere!

शब्दादिपञ्चकस्यास्य नैवासि त्वं न ते पुनः ।
त्वमेव परमं तत्त्वमतः किं परितप्यसे ॥ १६॥

shabdadi panchakasyasya naivasi tvam na te punah |
tvam eva paramam tattvamatah kim paritapyase ||1-16||

Where are the five senses such as hearing here? You do not belong to them, nor they to you. You are indeed the ultimate Reality! Why then, do you need penance?

जन्म मृत्युर्न ते चित्तं बन्धमोक्षौ शुभाशुभौ ।
कथं रोदिषि रे वत्स नामरूपं न ते न मे ॥ १७॥

janma murtyuh na te chittam bandha mokshas shubhashubhau |
katham rodishi re vatsa nama rupam na te na me ||1-17||

Birth and death have no power to stay in your consciousness, nor do bondage and liberation, nor good and bad. Why then, do you grieve, my child? You and I have no name or form!

अहो चित्त कथं भ्रान्तः प्रधावसि पिशाचवत् ।
अभिन्नं पश्य चात्मानं रागत्यागात्सुखी भव ॥ १८॥

aho chitta katham bhrantah pradhavasi pishachavat |
abhinnam pashya chatmanam raga-tyagat sukhi bhava ||1-18||

O mind, why do you wander and run around like a ghost? Know the Self as indivisible, abandon your passions, and be happy!

त्वमेव तत्त्वं हि विकारवर्जितं निष्कम्पमेकं हि विमोक्षविग्रहम् ।
न ते च रागो ह्यथवा विरागः कथं हि सन्तप्यसि कामकामतः ॥ १९॥

tvam eva tattvam hi vikaravarjitam niskampam ekam hi vimokshavigraham |
na te cha rago hyatha va viragah katham hi santapyasi kamakamatah ||1-19||

You are indeed the never-changing essence, immovable unity, totally free and formless! Neither attachment nor aversion are in you. How then, can you let the dictates of passion distress you so?

वदन्ति श्रुतयः सर्वाः निर्गुणं शुद्धमव्ययम् ।
अशरीरं समं तत्त्वं तन्मां विद्धि न संशयः ॥ २०॥

vadanti shrutayah sarvah nirjunam shuddham avyayam |
ashariram samam tattvam tan mam viddhi na samshayah ||1-20||

All the scriptures say Reality is pure, equanimous, imperishable, bodiless, beyond qualities. Realize this undifferentiated truth beyond doubt!

साकारमनृतं विद्धि निराकारं निरन्तरम् ।
एतत्तत्त्वोपदेशेन न पुनर्भवसम्भवः ॥ २१॥

sakaram anritam viddhi nirakaram nirantaram |
etat tatvopadeshena na punarbhava sambhavah ||1-21||

Realize that the essence of all forms is that which is formless and eternal! Once this truth is realized, there is no need for rebirth.

एकमेव रागं तत्त्वं वदन्ति हि विपश्चितः ।
रागत्यागात्पुनश्चित्तमेकानेकं न विद्यते ॥ २२॥

ekam eva samam tattvam vadanti hi vipashchitah |
raga-tyagat punah chittam ekanekam na vidyate ||1-22||

There is only one unequivocal truth, say the wise. Whether you keep or renounce attachments, consciousness remains one, never many!

अनात्मरूपं च कथं समाधि आत्मस्वरूपं च कथं समाधिः ।
अस्तीति नास्तीति कथं समाधि मोक्षस्वरूपं यदि सर्वमेकम् ॥ २३॥

anatmarupam cha katham samadhih atmasvarupam cha katham samadhih |
astiti nastiti katham samadhih mokshasvarupam yadi sarvam ekam ||1-23||

Where is deliverance in perceiving everything as external to Self? Where is deliverance in perceiving everything as the form of the Self? Where is deliverance in perceiving the Self as either existing or non-existing? Liberation is only in perceiving everything as One!

विशुद्धोऽसि समं तत्त्वं विदेहस्त्वमजोऽव्ययः ।
जानामीह न जानामीत्यात्मानं मन्यसे कथम् ॥ २४॥

vishuddhosi samam tattvam videhas tvam ajovyayah |
janamiha najanamit yatmanam manyase katham ||1-24||

You are pure, undifferentiated Reality, you have no body, no birth and no death. How then, can you believe 'I know the Self' or 'I do not know the Self?

तत्त्वमस्यादिवाक्येन स्वात्मा हि प्रतिपादितः ।
नेति नेति श्रुतिर्ब्रूयादनृतं पाञ्चभौतिकम् ॥ २५॥

tattvamasyadi vakyena svatma hi pratipaditah |
neti neti shrutir bruyat anritam panchabhautikam ||1-25||

Sayings such as 'Thou art That' explain the nature of your own Self, indeed. Sayings such as 'Not this, not this' show the unreality of the five elements.

आत्मन्येवात्मना सर्वं त्वया पूर्णं निरन्तरम् ।
ध्याता ध्यानं न ते चित्तं निर्लज्जं ध्यायते कथम् ॥ २६॥

atmanyevatmana sarvam tvaya purnam nirantaram |
dhyata dhyanam na te chittam nirlajjah dhyayate katham ||1-26||

The Self itself is the identity of everyone. You are complete and infinite; the differences between thinker and the thought do not belong to your consciousness at all. How then, can you shamelessly go on thinking so!

शिवं न जानामि कथं वदामि शिवं न जानामि कथं भजामि ।
अहं शिवश्चेत्परमार्थतत्त्वं समस्वरूपं गगनोपमं च ॥ २७॥

shivam na janami katham vadami shivam na janami katham bhajami |
aham shivash chet paramartha tattvam samasvarupam gaganopamam cha ||1-27||

I do not know Shiva, how can I speak of him? I do not know Shiva, how can I worship him? I myself am Shiva, the supreme Reality, ever the same, just like the sky!

नाहं तत्त्वं समं तत्त्वं कल्पनाहेतुवर्जितम् ।
ग्राह्यग्राहकनिर्मुक्तं स्वसंवेद्यं कथं भवेत् ॥ २८॥

naham tattvam samam tattvam kalpana hetu varjitam |
grahya grahaka hi muktam svasamvedyam katham bhavet ||1-28||

'I am not Reality', 'I am indeed, Reality' – I am beyond all such fanciful thoughts. I am beyond the perceiver and the perceived. How then, can I be the object of my own perception?

अनन्तरूपं न हि वस्तु किंचित्तत्त्वस्वरूपं न हि वस्तु किंचित् ।
आत्मैकरूपं परमार्थतत्त्वं न हिंसको वापि न चाप्यहिंसा ॥ २९॥

anantarupam na hi vastu kinchit tattvasvarupam na hi vastu kinchit |
atma ekarupam paramartha tattvam na hinsako vapi na cha apyahimsa ||1-29||

There is no such thing as 'the infinite form', there is no such thing as 'the real form'. The Self is the one and only form. It is not subject to death, and it cannot be killed.

विशुद्धोऽसि समं तत्त्वं विदेहमजमव्ययम् ।
विभ्रमं कथमात्मार्थे विभ्रान्तोऽहं कथं पुनः ॥ ३०॥

vishuddhosi samam tattvam videham ajam avyayam |
vibhramam katham atmarthe vibhrantoham katham punah ||1-30||

You are that pure, unchanging Reality. You have no body, no birth and no death. How then, can delusion exist for the Self? And how can the Self be deluded?

घटे भिन्ने घटाकाशं सुलीनं भेदवर्जितम् ।
शिवेन मनसा शुद्धो न भेदः प्रतिभाति मे ॥ ३१॥

ghate bhinne ghatakasham sulinam bheda varjitam |
shivena manasa shuddho na bhedah pratibhati me ||1-31||

When a pot is broken, the difference between the inside of the pot and the outside does not exist! Similarly, when the mind is purified in Shiva, there appears no duality to me!

न घटो न घटाकाशो न जीवो न जीवविग्रहः ।
केवलं ब्रह्म संविद्धि वेद्यवेदकवर्जितम् ॥ ३२॥

na ghato na ghatakasho na jivo jiva vigrahah |
kevalam brahma samviddhi vedya vedaka varjitam ||1-32||

In reality, there is no pot or space within, no body or soul within! Know that there is only one Brahman, who is beyond both the knower and the known!

सर्वत्र सर्वदा सर्वमात्मानं सततं ध्रुवम् ।
सर्वं शून्यमशून्यं च तन्मां विद्धि न संशयः ॥ ३३॥

sarvatra sarvada sarvam atmanam satatam dhruvam |
sarvam shunyam ashunyam cha tan mam viddhi na samshayah ||1-33||

Everywhere, eternally, in everything, only the Self is constant. Everything – nothingness or existence - is only my Self; I know this without doubt.

वेदा न लोका न सुरा न यज्ञा वर्णाश्रमो नैव कुलं न जातिः ।
न धूममार्गो न च दीप्तिमार्गो ब्रह्मैकरूपं परमार्थतत्त्वम् ॥ ३४॥

vedah na lokah na sura na yajnah varnashramo naiva kulam na jatih |
no dhuma-margo na cha diptimargo brahmaika rupam paramartha tattvam ||1-34||

There are no Vedas, no people, no gods, no sacrificial rites, no stages (ashramas) of life, neither castes nor creeds, neither smoky, unclear paths nor well-lit paths. There is only Brahman – the One Supreme Reality!

व्याप्यव्यापकनिर्मुक्तः त्वमेकः सफलं यदि ।
प्रत्यक्षं चापरोक्षं च ह्यात्मानं मन्यसे कथम् ॥ ३५॥

vyapya vyapaka nirmuktah tvam ekah saphalam yadi |
pratyaksham chaparoksam cha atmanam manyase katham ||1-35||

When you know that state of oneness which is beyond both subject and object, how can you believe the Self as either the observer or the observed?

अद्वैतं केचिदिच्छन्ति द्वैतमिच्छन्ति चापरे ।
समं तत्त्वं न विन्दन्ति द्वैताद्वैतविवर्जितम् ॥ ३६॥

advaitam kecid icchanti dvaitam icchanti chapare |
samam tattvam na vindanti dvaitadvaita vivarjitam ||1-36||

Some desire non-duality, others desire duality. They do not know the undifferentiated truth which is beyond both duality and non-duality.

श्वेतादिवर्णरहितं शब्दादिगुणवर्जितम् ।
कथयन्ति कथं तत्त्वं मनोवाचामगोचरम् ॥ ३७॥

shvetadivarna rahitam shabdadi guna varjitam |
kathayanti katham tattvam manovacham agocharam ||1-37||

It is beyond colours such as white, it is beyond qualities such as sound. What can one say about the Absolute Reality? It is far beyond both mind and speech.

यदाऽनृतमिदं सर्वं देहादिगगनोपमम् ।
तदा हि ब्रह्म संवेत्ति न ते द्वैतपरम्परा ॥ ३८॥

yadanritam idam sarvam dehadi gaganopamam |
tada hi brahma samvetti na te dvaita-parampara ||1-38||

When you understand how the body and all else is unreal and empty as the sky, then you know Brahman, and then you disown the entire tradition of duality.

परेण सहजात्मापि ह्यभिन्नः प्रतिभाति मे ।
व्योमाकारं तथैवैकं ध्याता ध्यानं कथं भवेत् ॥ ३९॥

parena sahajatmapi hyabhinnah pratibhati me |
vyomakaram tathaivaikam dhyata dhyanam katham bhavet ||1-39||

I perceive the innate nature of the Self as transcendental and undivided. Indeed, it is undivided like space! How, then, can the subject and object of meditation be two?

यत्करोमि यदश्नामि यज्जुहोमि ददामि यत् ।
एतत्सर्वं न मे किंचिद्विशुद्धोऽहमजोऽव्ययः ॥ ४०॥

yat karomi yad ashnami yajjuhomi dadami yat |
etat sarvam na me kim chit vishuddhoham ajovyayah ||1-40||

What I do, what I eat, what I sacrifice or give, none of this ever exists for me. I am purity itself, beyond birth and death!

सर्वं जगद्विद्धि निराकृतीदं सर्वं जगद्विद्धि विकारहीनम् ।
सर्वं जगद्विद्धि विशुद्धदेहं सर्वं जगद्विद्धि शिवैकरूपम् ॥ ४१॥

sarvam jagad viddhi nirakirtidam sarvam jagad viddhi vikarahinam |
sarvam jagad viddhi vishuddha deham sarvam jagad viddhi shivaikarupam ||1-41||

Know this entire universe is formless, know this entire universe is changeless. Know this entire universe is pure, know this entire universe is the singular form of Shiva!

तत्त्वं त्वं न हि सन्देहः किं जानाम्यथवा पुनः ।
असंवेद्यं स्वसंवेद्यमात्मानं मन्यसे कथम् ॥ ४२॥

tattvam tvam na hi sandhah kim janamyathava punah |
asamvedyam svasamvedyam atmanam manyase katham ||1-42||

You are the Absolute Reality, never doubt that or think 'How can I know it?' The Self knows the Self! How can you ever believe it is unknowable?

मायाऽमाया कथं तात छायाऽछाया न विद्यते ।
तत्त्वमेकमिदं सर्वं व्योमाकारं निरञ्जनम् ॥ ४३॥

maya amaya katham tata chhaya achhaya navidyate |
tattvam ekam idam sarvam vyomakaram niranjanam ||1-43||

Delusion or non-delusion? How could that be? Refuge or non-refuge? Those concepts do not exist! The only thing that exists is one, all-pervading, stainless Reality!

आदिमध्यान्तमुक्तोऽहं न बद्धोऽहं कदाचन ।
स्वभावनिर्मलः शुद्ध इति मे निश्चिता मतिः ॥ ४४॥

adi madhyanta muktoham na boddhoham kadachana |
svabhava nirmalas shuddhah iti me nischita matih ||1-44||

I am free of beginning, middle and end, I have never been bound. My nature is pure and stainless, I know this firmly.

महदादि जगत्सर्वं न किंचित्प्रतिभाति मे ।
ब्रह्मैव केवलं सर्वं कथं वर्णाश्रमस्थितिः ॥ ४५॥

mahad adi jagat sarvam na kim chit pratibhati me |
brahmaiva kevalam sarvam katham varnashrama sthitih ||1-45||

To me, the great expanse of this universe appears as nothing! Brahman alone is everything! Where then, are the stages (ashramas) of life?

जानामि सर्वथा सर्वमहमेकों निरन्तरम् ।
निरालम्बमशून्यं च शून्यं व्योमादिपञ्चकम् ॥ ४६॥

janami sarvatha sarvam eko tattva nirantaram |
niralambam ashunyam cha shunyam vyomadi panchakam ||1-46||

I always know everything as one, undivided reality. The world, the void, space, and the five elements – they are all One!

न षण्ढो न पुमान्न स्त्री न बोधो नैव कल्पना ।
सानन्दो वा निरानन्दमात्मानं मन्यसे कथम् ॥ ४७॥

na shandho na puman na stri na bodho naiva kalpana |
sanando va niranandam atmanam manyase katham ||1-47||

It is neither neuter, nor masculine, nor feminine. It has neither intellect nor imagination. How then, can you believe the Self is blissful or not blissful?

षडङ्गयोगान्न तु नैव शुद्धं मनोविनाशान्न तु नैव शुद्धम् ।
गुरूपदेशान्न तु नैव शुद्धं स्वयं च तत्त्वं स्वयमेव बुद्धम् ॥ ४८॥

shadanga yogan na tu naiva shuddham mano vinashan na tu naiva shuddham |
gurupadeshan na tu naiva shuddham svayam cha tattvam svayam eva buddham ||1-48||

Practicing six-limbed yoga will not purify you, conquering the mind will not purify you, a guru's teachings will not purify you. Purity is your very essence, it is your consciousness!

न हि पञ्चात्मको देहो विदेहो वर्तते न हि ।
आत्मैव केवलं सर्वं तुरीयं च त्रयं कथम् ॥ ४९॥

na hi panchatmako bhedo videho vartate na hi |
atmaiva kevalam sarvam turiyam cha trayam katham ||1-49||

Neither the physical body consisting of five elements, nor the subtle body exists. The Self alone is everything. Where then, is the fourth state of mind (pure consciousness) or the other three states (wakefulness, dreaming, deep sleep)?

न बद्धो नैव मुक्तोऽहं न चाहं ब्रह्मणः पृथक् ।
न कर्ता न च भोक्ताहं व्याप्यव्यापकवर्जितः ॥ ५०॥

na baddho naiva muktoham na chaham brahmanah prithak |
na karta na cha bhoktaham vyapya vyapaka varjitah ||1-50||

I am neither bound nor free. I am nothing other than Brahman. I am neither the doer, nor the experiencer, I beyond pervading or being pervaded.

यथा जलं जले न्यस्तं सलिलं भेदवर्जितम् ।
प्रकृतिं पुरुषं तद्वदभिन्नं प्रतिभाति मे ॥ ५१॥

yatha jalam jale nyastam salilam bheda varjitam |
prakritim purusham tadvad abhinnam pratibhati me ||1-51||

Just as when water is poured on water, there remains no distinction between the two different streams of water, similarly, I see no distinction between matter (Prakriti) and the consciousness (Purusha).

यदि नाम न मुक्तोऽसि न बद्धोऽसि कदाचन ।
साकारं च निराकारमात्मानं मन्यसे कथम् ॥ ५२॥

yadi nama na muktosi na baddhosi kadachana |
sakaram cha nirakaram atmanam manyase katham ||1-52||

If its identity is neither liberated nor bound, how can one think that the Self is either manifest or non-manifest?

जानामि ते परं रूपं प्रत्यक्षं गगनोपमम् ।
यथा परं हि रूपं यन्मरीचिजलसन्निभम् ॥ ५३॥

janami te param rupam pratyaksham gaganopamam |
yatha param hi rupam yan mariachi jala sannibham ||1-53||

I know that supreme One that extends everywhere like the sky. And it is that same supreme One that appears distorted like the water in a mirage.

न गुरुर्नोपदेशश्च न चोपाधिर्न मे क्रिया ।
विदेहं गगनं विद्धि विशुद्धोऽहं स्वभावतः ॥ ५४॥

na guruh na upadeshas cha na chopadhir na me kriya |
videham gaganam viddhi vishuddhoham svabhavatah ||1-54||

I have neither a guru, nor any teachings. I have no disciple and no duty. Know that I am formless like the sky, and pure by my very nature!

विशुद्धोऽस्य शरीरोऽसि न ते चित्तं परात्परम् ।
अहं चात्मा परं तत्त्वमिति वक्तुं न लज्जसे ॥ ५५॥

vishuddhosya shariro si na te chittam parat param |
aham chatma param tattvam iti vaktum na lajjase ||1-55||

You are pure, you have no body or mind, you are the most supreme of truths! "I am the Self, the supreme Reality!" - say this without shame!

कथं रोदिषि रे चित्त ह्यात्मैवात्मात्मना भव ।
पिब वत्स कलातीतमद्वैतं परमामृतम् ॥ ५६॥

katham rodishi re chitta hy atmaiva atmatmana bhava |
piba vatsa kalatitam advaitam paramamritam ||1-56||

Why do you weep, O mind? Decide yourself that 'I am the Self'. O child, drink the supreme nectar of Oneness, which surpasses all!

नैव बोधो न चाबोधो न बोधाबोध एव च ।
यस्येदृशः सदा बोधः स बोधो नान्यथा भवेत् ॥ ५७॥

naiva bodho na chobodho na bodhabodha eva cha |
yasyedrisah sada bodhah sa bodho nanyatha bhavet ||1-57||

You are neither intelligent, nor foolish, nor are you a mixture of the two. See yourself as pure, infinite intelligence, and nothing other than this intelligence!

ज्ञानं न तर्को न समाधियोगो न देशकालौ न गुरूपदेशः ।
स्वभावसंवित्तरहं च तत्त्वमाकाशकल्पं सहजं ध्रुवं च ॥ ५८॥

jnanam na tarko na samadhi yogo na desha kalau na gurupadeshah |
svabhava samvittaraham cha tattvam akasha kalpam sahajam dhruvam cha ||1-58||

I am neither in knowledge, nor in logic, nor in transcendental meditation, nor in any particular place or time, nor in the guru's teachings. Even though I appear scattered, I am the ultimate Reality, and my nature is innately constant like the sky!

न जातोऽहं मृतो वापि न मे कर्म शुभाशुभम् ।
विशुद्धं निर्गुणं ब्रह्म बन्धो मुक्तिः कथं मम ॥ ५९॥

na jatoham murto vapi na me karma shubhashubham |
vishuddham nirgunam brahma bandho muktih katham mama ||1-59||

I have no birth, no death, no duties, and have incurred no good or bad karma. I am pure Brahman, beyond all qualities. How can bondage or liberation exist for me?

यदि सर्वगतो देवः स्थिरः पूर्णो निरन्तरः ।
अन्तरं हि न पश्यामि स बाह्याभ्यन्तरः कथम् ॥ ६०॥

yadi sarvagato devah sthirah purnah nirantarah |
antaram hi na pashyami sabahyantarah hi katham ||1-60||

If God is all-pervading, unmoving, complete, constant, then I do not see any division in him at all! How can he be regarded as within or without?

स्फुरत्येव जगत्कृत्स्नमखण्डितनिरन्तरम् ।
अहो मायामहामोहो द्वैताद्वैतविकल्पना ॥ ६१॥

sphuratyeva jagat kirtsnam akhandita nirantaram |
aho maya maha moho dvaitadvaita vikalpana ||1-61||

The entire universe shines as an undivided constant! The concept of maya is a great delusion, and duality and non-duality are merely fancies!

साकारं च निराकारं नेति नेतीति सर्वदा ।
भेदाभेदविनिर्मुक्तो वर्तते केवलः शिवः ॥ ६२॥

sakaram cha nirakaram neti netiti sarvada |
bhedabheda vinirmukto vartate kevalah shivah ||1-62||

The manifest and the unmanifest – neither ever exist! Forever beyond the realm of union and separation, only Shiva alone exists!

न ते च माता च पिता च बन्धुः न ते च पत्नी न सुतश्च मित्रम् ।
न पक्षपाती न विपक्षपातः कथं हि संतप्तिरियं हि चित्ते ॥ ६३॥

na te cha mata cha pita cha bandhuh na te cha patni na sutas cha mitram |
na pakshapato na vipakshapatah katham hi santaptiriyam hi chitte ||1-63||

You have no mother, no father, no relative, no wife, no son or friend. You are neither partial, nor impartial to anything. Why then, do you carry such deep torment in your heart?

दिवा नक्तं न ते चित्तं उदयास्तमयौ न हि ।
विदेहस्य शरीरत्वं कल्पयन्ति कथं बुधाः ॥ ६४॥

diva naktam na te chittam udayastamayau na hi |
videhasya shariratvam kalpayanti katham budhah ||1-64||

There is neither day and night, nor rising and setting within your consciousness. How then, can the wise one ever imagine the formless as having a body?

नाविभक्तं विभक्तं च न हि दुःखसुखादि च ।
न हि सर्वमसर्वं च विद्धि चात्मानमव्ययम् ॥ ६५॥

na vibhaktam vibhaktam cha nahi duhkhasukhadi cha |
na hi sarvam asarvam cha viddhi chatmanam avyayam ||1-65||

Know the never-changing Self! It is neither undivided nor divided. It experiences neither joy nor sorrow nor anything else. It is not everything, nor is it nothing!

नाहं कर्ता न भोक्ता च न मे कर्म पुराऽधुना ।
न मे देहो विदेहो वा निर्ममेति ममेति किम् ॥ ६६॥

naham karta na bhokta cha na me karma puradhuna |
na me deho videho va nirmameti mameti kim ||1-66||

I am neither the doer, nor the experiencer. I have no karma, either in the past or in the present. I am neither with nor without a body. What then, is 'mine' or 'not mine'?

न मे रागादिको दोषो दुःखं देहादिकं न मे ।
आत्मानं विद्दि मामेकं विशालं गगनोपमम् ॥ ६७॥

na me ragadiko dosho duhkham dehadikam na me |
atmanam viddhi mam ekam vishalam gaganopamam ||1-67||

There is no attachment or other fault in me, there is no pain in the body or elsewhere for me. I only know I am the One Self, vast as the sky!

सखे मनः किं बहुजल्पितेन सखे मनः सर्वमिदं वितर्क्यम् ।
यत्सारभूतं कथितं मया ते त्वमेव तत्त्वं गगनोपमोऽसि ॥ ६८॥

sakhe manah kim bahu jalpitena sakhe manah sarvam idam vitarkyam |
yat sara-bhutam kathitam maya te tvam eva tattvam gaganopamosi ||1-68||

O mind, my friend, why cling to things so much? O mind, my friend, everything that you see is doubtful! I have told you the essence of the truth. You yourself are the ultimate Reality, free as the sky!

येन केनापि भावेन यत्र कुत्र मृता अपि ।
योगिनस्तत्र लीयन्ते घटाकाशमिवाम्बरे ॥ ६९॥

yena kenapi bhavena yatra kutra murta api |
yoginah tatra liyante ghatakasham ivambare ||1-69||

Wherever or in whatever state a yogi dies, he becomes absorbed into the Absolute, just as the space within a pot becomes absorbed into outer space when the pot is broken.

तीर्थे चान्त्यजगेहे वा नष्टस्मृतिरपि त्यजन् ।
समकाले तनुं मुक्तः कैवल्यव्यापको भवेत् ॥ ७० ॥

tirthe chantyajagehe va nashtasmrutih api tyajan |
samakale tanum muktah kaivalyavyapako bhavet ||1-70||

Whether he quits his body at a holy place of pilgrimage, or at a degenerate place, or with his memory totally lost - at the time of death, he merges into freedom, into Absolute Unity!

धर्मार्थकाममोक्षांश्च द्विपदादिचराचरम् ।
मन्यन्ते योगिनः सर्वं मरीचिजलसन्निभम् ॥ ७१ ॥

dharmartha karma mokshams cha dvipadadi characharam |
manyante yoginah sarvam marichi jala sannibham ||1-71||

Righteousness, wealth, desire, liberation, people, all moving and stationary things in the world – the yogi believes all these to be illusory, like water in a mirage.

अतीतानागतं कर्म वर्तमानं तथैव च ।
न करोमि न भुञ्जामि इति मे निश्चला मतिः ॥ ७२ ॥

atitanagatam karma vartamanam tathaiva cha |
na karomi na bhunjami iti me nishchala matih ||1-72||

There is no action in the past, present or future that has been performed or experienced by me. I know this without a doubt.

शून्यागारे समरसपूत- स्तिष्ठन्नेकः सुखमवधूतः ।
चरति हि नग्नस्त्यक्त्वा गर्वं विन्दति केवलमात्मनि सर्वम् ॥ ७३ ॥

shunyagare samarasa putah tishthan nekah sukham avadhutah |
charati hi nagnah tyaktva garvam vindati kevalam atmani
sarvam ||1-73||

The Avadhuta stays alone and happy in a deserted place, pure and with an equanimous mind. Knowing everything is the Self, he surrenders pride and roams about naked!

त्रितयतुरीयं नहि नहि यत्र विन्दति केवलमात्मनि तत्र ।
धर्माधर्मौ नहि नहि यत्र बद्धो मुक्तः कथमिह तत्र ॥ ७४॥

tritaya turiyam nahi nahi yatra vindati kevalam atmani tatra |
dharmadharmo nahi nahi yatra baddho muktah katham iha
tatra ||1-74||

Where there is no third state (deep sleep) or the fourth state (pure consciousness), only the Self exists! Where there is no righteousness or non-righteousness, where there is no bondage or liberation, how can this world exist!

विन्दति विन्दति नहि नहि यत्रं छन्दोलक्षणं नहि नहि तत्रं ।
समरसमग्नो भावितपूतः प्रलपितमेतत्परमवधूतः ॥ ७५॥

vindati vindati nahi nahi yatram chhandolakshanam nahi nahi
tatram |
samarasa magno bhavita putah pralapitam etat param
avadhutah ||1-75||

Where there is no knowing even upon knowing, there are no scriptures or diverse knowledge. Deeply immersed in equanimity, purified and in the highest spiritual state, I, the Avadhuta, thus speak of the Absolute Reality!

सर्वशून्यमशून्यं च सत्यासत्यं न विद्यते ।
स्वभावभावतः प्रोक्तं शास्त्रसंवित्तिपूर्वकम् ॥ ७६ ॥

sarvashunyam ashunyam cha satya asatyam na vidyate |
svabhava bhavatah proktam shastra samvitti purvakam ||1-76||

Neither nothing nor everything exists, neither truth nor falsehood exists. All scriptures in agreement assert that there exists only Self-nature!

iti shri dattatreya virachitayam avadhuta gitayam atma samvittiupadesho nama prathamodhyayah ||

In this Song of the Avadhuta composed by Shri Dattatreya, this is the first chapter on the teaching of the wisdom of the Self.

Chapter 2

अथ द्वितीयोऽध्यायः ।
atha dvitiya adhyayah |
Second Adhyaya

बालस्य वा विषयभोगरतस्य वापि मूर्खस्य सेवकजनस्य गृहस्थितस्य ।
एतद्गुरोः किमपि नैव न चिन्तनीयं रत्नं कथं त्यजति कोऽप्यशुचौ
प्रविष्टम् ॥ १॥

balasya va vishayabhoga ratasya vapi murkhasya sevaka janasya gruhasthitasya |
etadguroh kim api naiva vichintaniyam ratnam katham tyajati kopyashuchau pravishtam ||2-1||

You may be young, addicted to sensual pleasures, foolish, a servant or a householder. When does a jewel need a guru to be valuable? When is it ever thrown away in anger just because it is covered in mud?

नैवात्र काव्यगुण एव तु चिन्तनीयो ग्राह्यः परं गुणवता खलु सार एव ।
सिन्दूरचित्ररहिता भुवि रूपशून्या पारं न किं नयति नौरिह
गन्तुकामान् ॥ २॥

naivatra kavyaguna eva tu chintaniyo grahyah param gunavata khalu sara eva |
sindura chitra rahita bhuvi rupashunya param na kim nayati nauriha gantu kaman ||2-2||

You may consider yourself unskilled in literature, but know that the true essence is beyond such qualities! When you really want to go across, even an unpainted, undecorated, unattractive boat will take you!

प्रयत्नेन विना येन निश्चलेन चलाचलम् ।
ग्रस्तं स्वभावतः शान्तं चैतन्यं गगनोपमम् ॥ ३॥

prayatnena vina yena nishchalena chalachalam |
grastam svabhavatah shantam chaitanyam gaganopamam ||2-3||

The Self appears as both deliberate and unintentional, both animate and inanimate. It is always absorbed in its own tranquil natural state. It is pure consciousness, vast as the sky!

अयत्नाच्छालयेद्यस्तु एकमेव चराचरम् ।
सर्वगं तत्कथं भिन्नमद्वैतं वर्तते मम ॥ ४॥

ayatnat chalayed yastu ekam eva chacharam |
sarvagam tat katham bhinnam advaitam vartate mama ||2-4||

It effortlessly appears as either inaminate or animate, but it is One and all-pervading! Where then, is duality? There is only unity in me!

अहमेव परं यस्मात्सारात्सारतरं शिवम् ।
गमागमविनिर्मुक्तं निर्विकल्पं निराकुलम् ॥ ५॥

aham eva param yasmat sarat sarataram shivam |
gamagama vinirmuktam nirvikalpam nirakulam ||2-5||

I am that which is supreme, the essence of all essences, I am Shiva! I am beyond coming and going, I am without imagination, I am unperturbed.

सर्वावयवनिर्मुक्तं तथाहं त्रिदशार्चितम् ।
संपूर्णत्वान्न गृह्णामि विभागं त्रिदशादिकम् ॥ ६॥

sarvavaya vanirmuktam tathaham tridasha architam |
sampurnatvan na gruhanami vibhagam tridashadikam ||2-6||

I am beyond all my component parts. Therefore, even though thirty gods may worship me, I do not accept any divisions, such as thirty gods, within my perfect completeness!

प्रमादेन न सन्देहः किं करिष्यामि वृत्तिमान् ।
उत्पद्यन्ते विलीयन्ते बुद्बुदाश्च यथा जले ॥ ७॥

parmadena na sandehah kim karisyami vrittivan |
utpadyante viliyante budbudah cha yatha jale ||2-7||

Neither foolishness nor doubt can have any impact on my nature. They are like bubbles rising and subsiding in water.

महदादीनि भूतानि समाप्यैवं सदैव हि ।
मृदुद्रव्येषु तीक्ष्णेषु गुडेषु कटुकेषु च ॥ ८॥

mahadadini bhutani samapyaivam sadaiva hi |
murdudravyeshu tikshneshu gudeshu katukeshu cha ||2-8||

The numerous material elements that compose the material world are always finite, including all things that are soft, sharp, sweet or bitter.

कटुत्वं चैव शैत्यत्वं मृदुत्वं च यथा जले ।
प्रकृतिः पुरुषस्तद्वदभिन्नं प्रतिभाति मे ॥ ९॥

katutvam chaiva shaityatvam mrudutvam cha yatha jale |
prakritih purushah tadvat abhinnam pratibhati me ||2-9||

Bitterness, coldness, softness – are all qualities of water. Similarly, material nature (Prakriti) and consciousness (Purusha) are my undifferentiated qualities.

सर्वाख्यारहितं यद्यत्सूक्ष्मात्सूक्ष्मतरं परम् ।
मनोबुद्धीन्द्रियातीतमकलङ्कं जगत्पतिम् ॥ १०॥

sarvakhya rahitam yad yat sukshmat sukshmataram param |
manobuddhi indriyatitam akalankam jagatpatim ||2 10||

Free of all names, beyond the subtlest of the subtle, transcending the mind, the intellect and the senses – such is the stainless one – the lord of the universe!

ईदृशं सहजं यत्र अहं तत्र कथं भवेत् ।
त्वमेव हि कथं तत्र कथं तत्र चराचरम् ॥ ११॥

idrasham sahajam yatra aham tatra katham bhavet |
tvam evahi katham tatra katham tatra characharam ||2-11||

When such is the original state, then how can there be an "I"? How can there be a "You"? How can there be animate and inanimate things?

गगनोपमं तु यत्प्रोक्तं तदेव गगनोपमम् ।
चैतन्यं दोषहीनं च सर्वज्ञं पूर्णमेव च ॥ १२॥

gaganopamam tu yat proktam tad eva gaganopamam |
chaitanyam doshahinam cha sarvajnam purnam eva cha ||2-12||

What is said to be like the sky is indeed like the sky. It is pure consciousness, without faults, all-knowing, complete.

पृथिव्यां चरितं नैव मारुतेन च वाहितम् ।
वरिणा पिहितं नैव तेजोमध्ये व्यवस्थितम् ॥ १३॥

prithivyam charitam naiva marutena cha vahitam |
varina pihitam naiva tejomadhye vyavasthitam ||2-13||

It does not walk on land, it does not blow in the wind, it does not drown in water, nor is it situated in the midst of fire.

आकाशं तेन संव्याप्तं न तद्व्याप्तं च केनचित् ।
स बाह्याभ्यन्तरं तिष्ठत्यवच्छिन्नं निरन्तरम् ॥ १४॥

akasham tena samvyaptam na tad vyaptam cha kenachit |
sa bahyabhyantaram tishthat yavat chhinnam nirantaram ||2-14||

Space is pervaded by it, but it is not pervaded by anything. It stands both within and without, it is indivisible and infinite.

सूक्ष्मत्वात्तदद‌ृश्यत्वान्निर्गुणत्वाच्च योगिभिः ।
आलम्बनादि यत्प्रोक्तं क्रमादालम्बनं भवेत् ॥ १५॥

suksmatvat tad adrashyatvat nirgunatvat cha yogibhih |
alambanadi yat proktam kramad alambanam bhavet ||2-15||

It is very subtle, it is invisible, it is beyond qualities, say the yogis. It is the foundation, it is said, on which all other things come to rest in due course.

सतताऽभ्यासयुक्तस्तु निरालम्बो यदा भवेत् ।
तल्लयाल्लीयते नान्तर्गुणदोषविवर्जितः ॥ १६॥

satata abhyasa yuktastu niralambo yada bhavet |
tad layat liyate na antar gunadosha vivarjitah ||2-16||

When one practices being established in the Self continuously, then one becomes non-attached. Thus absorbed in the Self, one goes beyond the faults of all qualities (gunas).

विषाविश्वस्य रौद्रस्य मोहगूर्च्छाप्रदस्य च ।
एकमेव विनाशाय ह्यमोघं सहजामृतम् ॥ १७॥

visha vishvasya raudrasya moha murcha pradasya cha |
ekam eva vinashaya hyamogham sahajamritam ||2-17||

The vicious, withering poison of lust and infatuation with the world can be destroyed by only one antidote – the nectar of the original nature!

भावगम्यं निराकारं साकारं दृष्टिगोचरम् ।
भावाभावविनिर्मुक्तमन्तरालं तदुच्यते ॥ १८॥

bhava gamyam nirakaram sakaram drishti gocharam |
bhavabhava vinirmuktam antaralam tad uchyate ||2-18||

Unmanifest states cannot be perceived by the mind, only manifest states are perceived by the eye. But what is beyond both manifest and unmanifest states is known as the inner Self.

बाह्यभावं भवेद्विश्वमन्तः प्रकृतिरुच्यते ।
अन्तरादन्तरं ज्ञेयं नारिकेलफलाम्बुवत् ॥ १९॥

bahya bhavam bhaved vishvam antah prakritir uchyate |
antaradantaram jneyam narikela phalambuvat ||2-19||

The state experienced without takes the form of the universe, the state experienced within takes the form of nature. But know deep in the inner core of the inner state, is the real milk of the coconut (pure consciousness).

भ्रान्तिज्ञानं स्थितं बाह्यं सम्यग्ज्ञानं च मध्यगम् ।
मध्यान्मध्यतरं ज्ञेयं नारिकेलफलाम्बुवत् ॥ २०॥

bhranti jnanam sthitam bahyam samyagnanam cha madhyagam |
madhyan madhyataram gneyam narikela phalambuvat ||2-20||

Various diversified knowledge is the outer shell, equanimous self-knowledge is the middle, and in the core of the centre is the real milk of the coconut (pure consciousness).

पौर्णमास्यां यथा चन्द्र एक एवातिनिर्मलः ।
तेन तत्सदृशं पश्येद्द्विधादृष्टिविपर्ययः ॥ २१॥

paurnamasyam yatha chandra eka evatinirmalah |
tena tat sadrisham pashyet bheda drishtih viparyayah ||2-21||

Just as the moon appears as one and resplendent on a full-moon night, so should Reality be seen as one. A sight that perceives division is faulty.

अनेनैव प्रकारेण बुद्धिभेदो न सर्वगः ।
दाता च धीरतामेति गीयते नामकोटिभिः ॥ २२॥

anenaiva prakarena buddhi bhedo na sarvagah |
data cha dhiratam eti giyate namakotibhih ||2-22||

The perception of many is an aberration of the mind, Reality is one, not many. The one who is purified with this wisdom deserves to be praised a thousand times.

गुरुप्रज्ञाप्रसादेन मूर्खो वा यदि पण्डितः ।
यस्तु संबुध्यते तत्त्वं विरक्तो भवसागरात् ॥ २३॥

gurupragna prasadena murkho va yadi panditah |
yastu sambudhyate tattvam virakto bhava sagarat ||2-23||

A guru gives the prasada of wisdom to everyone, be he foolish or learned. But only he crosses over this ocean of existence, who learns the truth for himself.

रागद्वेषविनिर्मुक्तः सर्वभूतहिते रतः ।
दृढबोधश्च धीरश्च स गच्छेत्परमं पदम् ॥ २४॥

ragadvesha vinirmuktah sarvabhuta hite ratah |
dradha bodhah cha dhirah cha sa gacchet paramam padam ||2-24||

He who is free from attraction and repulsion, who is engaged in doing good for all, who is firmly determined and wise, he attains the supreme state.

घटे भिन्ने घटाकाश आकाशे लीयते यथा ।
देहाभावे तथा योगी स्वरूपे परमात्मनि ॥ २५॥

ghate bhinne ghatakasha akashe liyate yatha |
dehabhave tatha yogi svarupe paramatmani ||2-25||

When a pot breaks, the space inside merges into the space outside. Similarly, when a yogi quits his body, he becomes one with his true Self – the supreme universal consciousness.

उक्तेयं कर्मयुक्तानां मतिर्यान्तेऽपि सा गतिः ।
न चोक्ता योगयुक्तानां मतिर्यान्तेऽपि सा गतिः ॥ २६॥

ukteyam karma yuktanam matiryantepi sa gatih |
na chokta yoga yuktanam matiryantepi sa gatih ||2-26||

It is said the destiny of those who are devoted to action is decided by their state of mind at the end of their life. But the destiny of the one established in yoga is not determined by his state of mind at the end.

या गतिः कर्मयुक्तानां सा च वागिन्द्रियाद्वदेत् ।
योगिनां या गतिः क्वापि ह्यकथ्या भवतोर्जिता ॥ २७॥

ya gatih karmayuktanam sa cha vag indriyad vadet |
yoginam ya gatih kvapi hyakathya bhavatorjita ||2-27||

The destiny of those devoted to action can be expressed with speech. But how to describe the destiny of the yogi? It is beyond expression.

एवं ज्ञात्वा त्वमुं मार्गं योगिनां नैव कल्पितम् ।
विकल्पवर्जनं तेषां स्वयं सिद्धिः प्रवर्तते ॥ २८॥

evam gnatva tvamum margam yoginam naiva kalpitam |
vikalpa varjanam tesham svayam siddhih pravartate ||2-28||

A yogi does not imagine knowing any particular path, he simply ceases to imagine! In this state, perfection naturally occurs!

तीर्थे वान्त्यजगेहे वा यत्र कुत्र मृतोऽपि वा ।
न योगी पश्यते गर्भं परे ब्रह्मणि लीयते ॥ २९॥

tirthe va antyaja gehe va yatra kutra murtopi va |
na yogi pashyate garbham pare bruhmuni liyate ||2-29||

Wherever a yogi dies – whether it is at a place of pilgrimage or at an immoral place, he does not take birth again. He merges into the Absolute.

सहजमजमचिन्त्यं यस्तु पश्येत्स्वरूपं घटति यदि यथेष्टं लिप्यते नैव दोषैः ।
सकृदपि तदभावात्कर्म किंचिन्नकुर्यात् तदपि न च विबद्धः संयमी वा तपस्वी ॥ ३०॥

sahajam ajam achintyam yastu pashyet svarupam ghatati yadi yatheshtam lipyate naiva doshaih |
sakrud api tadabhavat karma kinchit na kuryat tadapi na cha vibaddhah sanyami va tapasvi ||2-30||

When one realizes the Self which is innate, unborn and inconceivable, faults cannot cling even when one continues to be occupied according to one's own nature. The disciplined ascetic's conduct is always benevolent. He is always free of karma, and he is never bound.

निरामयं निष्प्रतिमं निराकृतिं निराश्रयं निर्वपुषं निराशिषम् ।
निर्द्वन्द्वनिर्मोहमलुप्तशक्तिकं तमीशमात्मानमुपैति शाश्वतम् ॥ ३१॥

niramayam nishpratimam nirakrutim nirashrayam nirvapusham nirashisham |
nirdvandva nirmoham alupta shaktikam tam isham atmanam upaiti shashvatam ||2-31||

Free of illness, free of illusion, free of form, free of dependence, free of bodily obsession, free of hope, free of duality, free of desire, free of power - he attains God, the Self, the Eternal!

वेदो न दीक्षा न च मुण्डनक्रिया गुरुर्न शिष्यो न च यत्रसम्पदः ।
मुद्रादिकं चापि न यत्र भासते तमीशमात्मानमुपैति शाश्वतम् ॥ ३२॥

vedo na diksha na cha mundane kriya gururna shishyo na cha yatra sampadah |
mudradikam chapi na yatra bhasate tam isham atmanam upaiti shashvatam ||2-32||

Neither the Vedas nor initiation, nor a ceremonially shaved head; neither guru nor disciple; neither possessions nor wealth - he attains God, the Self, the Eternal!

न शाम्भवं शक्तिकमानवं न वा पिण्डं च रूपं च पदादिकं न वा ।
आरम्भनिष्पत्तिघटादिकं च नो तमीशमात्मानमुपैति शाश्वतम् ॥ ३३॥

na shambhavam shaktika manavam na va pindam cha rupam cho padadikam na va |
arambha nishpatti ghatadikam cha no tam isham atmanam upaiti shashvatam ||2-33||

Neither the great Shiva nor goddess Shakti nor human beings; neither the solid form nor the feet of God; neither beginning, nor climax, nor descension - he attains God, the Self, the Eternal!

यस्य स्वरूपात्सचराचरं जगदुत्पद्यते तिष्ठति लीयतेऽपि वा ।
पयोविकारादिव फेनबुद्बुदास्तमीशमात्मानमुपैति शाश्वतम् ॥ ३४॥

yasya svarupat sacharacharam jagad utpadyate tishthati liyatepi va |
payo vikarad iva phena budbudah tam isham atmanam upaiti shashvatam ||2-34||

That fundamental nature from which the animate and inanimate world is born, on which it stands, and into which it ultimately merges, like the change in the state of foam and bubbles when milk is shaken or kept still – he attains (that nature of), God, the Self, the Eternal!

नासानिरोधो न च दृष्टिरासनं बोधोऽप्यबोधोऽपि न यत्र भासते ।
नाडीप्रचारोऽपि न यत्र किञ्चित्तमीशमात्मानमुपैति शाश्वतम् ॥ ३५॥

nasa nirodho na cha drishtih asanam bodho apyabodhopi na yatra bhasate |
nadi pracharopi na yatra kinchit tam isham atmanam upaiti shashvatam ||2-35||

The state where there is neither holding of breath nor curbing of visual enjoyment; neither perceiving wisdom nor foolishness, nor studying of nerve patterns – he attains (that state of) God, the Self, the Eternal!

नानात्वमेकत्वमुभत्वमन्यता अणुत्वदीर्घत्वमहत्त्वशून्यता ।
मानत्वमेयत्वसमत्ववर्जितं तमीशमात्मानमुपैति शाश्वतम् ॥ ३६॥

nanatvam ekatvam ubhatvam anyata anutva dirghatva mahatva shunyata |
manatva meyatva samatva varjitam tam isham atmanam upaiti shashvatam ||2-36||

What is beyond 'one-ness', 'two-ness', 'many-ness' or manifoldness, beyond minusculeness or expansiveness, beyond greatness or nothingness, beyond measurability, quantification or comparison – he attains (that state of) God, the Self, the Eternal!

सुसंयमी वा यदि वा न संयमी सुसंग्रही वा यदि वा न संग्रही ।
निष्कर्मको वा यदि वा सकर्मक-स्तमीशमात्मानमुपैति शाश्वतम् ॥ ३७॥

susanyami va yadi va na sanyami susangrahi va yadi va na sangrahi |
nishkarmako va yadi va sakarmakastam isham atmanam upaiti shashvatam ||2-37||

Whether he is disciplined or undisciplined, whether he clings to senses or is free of them, whether he clings to actions or is free of them – he attains God, the Self, the Eternal!

मनो न बुद्धिर्न शरीरमिन्द्रियं तन्मात्रभूतानि न भूतपञ्चकम् ।
अहंकृतिश्चापि वियत्स्वरूपकं तमीशमात्मानमुपैति शाश्वतम् ॥ ३८॥

mano na buddhih na shariram indriyam tanmatra bhutani na bhuta panchakam |
ahamkrutih cha api viyat svarupakam tam isham atmanam upaiti shashvatam ||2-38||

Neither the mind, nor the intellect, nor the body, nor the senses; neither the subtle elements nor the five gross elements; neither ego nor the subtle body – he attains God, the Self, the Eternal!

विधौ निरोधे परमात्मतां गते न योगिनश्चेतसि भेदवर्जिते ।
शौचं न वाशौचमलिङ्गभावना सर्वं विधेयं यदि वा निषिध्यते ॥ ३९॥

vidhau nirodhe paramatmatam gate na yoginah chetasi bhedavarjite |
shaucham na vashaucham alingabhavana sarvam vidheyam yadi va nishidhyate ||2-39||

Rejecting all precepts, he rests in the supreme Self. Thus, the consciousness of the yogi becomes free of duality. Purity or impurity, expressing lust or restricting everything – these have no meaning for him.

मनो वचो यत्र न शक्तमीरितुं नूनं कथं तत्र गुरूपदेशता ।
इमां कथामुक्तवतो गुरोस्तद्युक्तस्य तत्त्वं हि समं प्रकाशते ॥ ४०॥

mano vacho yatra na shaktam iritum nunam katham tatra guru upadeshata |
imam katham uktavato guroh tad yuktasya tattvam hi samam prakashate ||2-40||

What the mind or speech are not able to express, indeed, how can a guru's teachings express that? How can a guru say anything about that primordial essence which illuminates everything!

shri dattatreya virachitayam avadhuta gitayam atma samvittyupadesho nama dvitiyodhyayah ||

In this Song of the Avadhuta composed by Shri Dattatreya, this is the second chapter on the teaching of the wisdom of the Self.

Chapter 3

अथ तृतीयोऽध्यायः ।
atha trutiya adhyayah |
Third Adhyaya

गुणविगुणविभागो वर्तते नैव किञ्चित् रतिविरतिविहीनं निर्मलं निष्प्रपञ्चम् ।
गुणविगुणविहीनं व्यापकं विश्वरूपं कथमहमिह वन्दे व्योमरूपं शिवं वै ॥ १॥

guna viguna vibhago vartate naiva kinchit rati virati vihinam nirmalam nishprapancham |
guna viguna vihinam vyapakam vishvarupam katham aham iha vande vyomarupam shivam vai ||3-1||

For him, there is no distinction between being with qualities or without. He is beyond both attachment and non-attachment, he is stainless and uncomplicated. Beyond both good and bad qualities, he permeates the entire universe! How do I worship that Shiva, who is formless like space!

श्वेतादिवर्णरहितो नियतं शिवश्च कार्यं हि कारणमिदं हि परं शिवश्च ।
एवं विकल्परहितोऽहमलं शिवश्च स्वात्मानमात्मनि सुमित्र कथं
नमामि ॥ २॥

shvetadi varna rahito niyatam shivah cha karyam hi karanam idam hi param shivah cha |
evam vikalpa rahito aham alam shivah cha sva atmanam atmani sumitra katham namami ||3-2||

Shiva is always beyond colours such as white, Shiva is beyond both cause and effect. Truly, I am Shiva, beyond imagination! My friend, how do I myself bow down to myself?

निर्मूलमूलरहितो हि सदोदितोऽहं निर्धूमधूमरहितो हि सदोदितोऽहम् ।
निर्दीपदीपरहितो हि सदोदितोऽहं ज्ञानामृतं समरसं गगनोपमोऽहम् ॥ ३॥

nirmula mula rahito hi sadoditoham nirdhuma dhuma rahito hi sadoditoham |
nirdipa dipa rahito hi sadoditoham gnanamrutam samarasam gaganopamoham ||3-3||

Beyond pointedness or pointlessness, I am an ever-rising sun! Beyond smoky obscurity or clarity, I am an ever-rising sun! Beyond light and darkness, I am an ever-rising sun! I am the nectar of knowledge, I am equanimous bliss, I am vast as space!

निष्कामकाममिह नाम कथं वदामि निःसङ्गसङ्गमिह नाम कथं वदामि ।
निःसारसाररहितं च कथं वदामि ज्ञानामृतं समरसं गगनोपमोऽहम् ॥ ४॥

niskama kamam iha nama katham vadami nihsanga sangam iha nama katham vadami |

44

nihsara sara rahitam cha katham vadami gnanamrutam samarasam gaganopamoham ||3-4||

Desire, desirelessness – now how do I define these concepts? Attachment, non-attachment – now how do I define these concepts? Pointlessness, pointedness – now how do I define these concepts? I am the nectar of knowledge, I am equanimous bliss, I am vast as space!

अद्वैतरूपमखिलं हि कथं वदामि द्वैतस्वरूपमखिलं हि कथं वदामि ।
नित्यं त्वनित्यमखिलं हि कथं वदामि ज्ञानामृतं समरसं
गगनोपमोऽहम् ॥ ५॥

advaita rupam akhilam hi katham vadami dvaita svarupam akhilam hi katham vadami |
nityam tvanityam akhilam hi katham vadami gnanamrutam samarasam gaganopamoham ||3-5||

How do I define the absolute concept of non-duality? How do I define the absolute concept of duality? How do I define absolute eternity and non-eternity? I am the nectar of knowledge, I am equanimous bliss, I am vast as space!

स्थूलं हि नो नहि कृशं न गतागतं हि आद्यन्तमध्यरहितं न परापरं हि ।
सत्यं वदामि खलु वै परमार्थतत्त्व ज्ञानामृत समरस गगनोपमोऽहम् ॥ ६॥

sthulam hi no nahi krusham na gatagatam hi adianta Madhya rahitam na paraparam hi |
satyam vadami khalu vai paramartha tattvam gnanamrutam samarasam gaganopamoham ||3-6||

I am neither gross nor subtle, I neither come nor go. I am free of beginning, middle and end, I am neither superior nor inferior. Indeed, I speak only the truth about the supreme Reality. I am the nectar of knowledge, I am equanimous bliss, I am vast as space!

संविद्धि सर्वकरणानि नभोनिभानि संविद्धि सर्वविषयांश्च नभोनिभांश्च ।
संविद्धि चैकममलं न हि बन्धमुक्तं ज्ञानामृतं समरसं गगनोपमोऽहम् ॥ ७॥

samviddhi sarva karanani nabho nibhani samviddhi sarva vishayan cha nabho nibhan cha |
samviddhi cha ekam amalam na hi bandha muktam gnanamrutam samarasam gaganopamoham ||3-7||

Know that all sense organs are empty as the sky, know that all sense objects are also empty as the sky. Know that there is only one stainless One that is neither liberated nor bound – I am that nectar of knowledge, I am equanimous bliss, I am vast as space!

दुर्बोधबोधगहनो न भवामि तात दुर्लक्ष्यलक्ष्यगहनो न भवामि तात ।
आसन्नरूपगहनो न भवामि तात ज्ञानामृतं समरसं गगनोपमोऽहम् ॥ ८॥

durbodha bodha gahano na bhavami tata durlakshya lakshya gahano na bhavami tata |
asanna rupa gahano na bhavami tata gnanamrutam samarasam gaganopamoham ||3-8||

I am unfathomable, inaccessible via intellect - intellect cannot define me. I am imperceptible, inaccessible via sight - sight cannot define me. I am not solid, unlimited by form - form cannot define me. I am the nectar of knowledge, I am equanimous bliss, I am vast as space!

निष्कर्मकर्मदहनो ज्वलनो भवामि निर्दुःखदुःखदहनो ज्वलनो भवामि ।
निर्देहदेहदहनो ज्वलनो भवामि ज्ञानामृतं समरसं गगनोपमोऽहम् ॥ ९॥

nishkarma karma dahano jvalano bhavami nirduhkha duhkha dahano jvalano bhavami |
nirdeha deha dahano jvalano bhavami gnanamrutam samarasam gaganopamoham ||3-9||

I am without karma, I am the fire in which all karma is consumed. I am without sorrow, I am the fire in which all sorrow is consumed. I am without body, I am the fire in which all forms are consumed. I am the nectar of knowledge, I am equanimous bliss, I am vast as space!

निष्पापपापदहनो हि हुताशनोऽहं निर्धर्मधर्मदहनो हि हुताशनोऽहम् ।
निर्बन्धबन्धदहनो हि हुताशनोऽहं ज्ञानामृतं समरसं गगनोपमोऽहम् ॥ १०॥

nishpapa papa dahano hi hutashanoham nirdharma dharma dahano hi hutashanoham |
nirbandha bandha dahano hi hutashanoham gnanamrutam samarasam gaganopamoham ||3-10||

I am sinless, I am the fire in which all sins are consumed. I am dutiless, I am the fire in which all duties are consumed. I am unbound, I am the fire in which all bondage is consumed. I am the nectar of knowledge, I am equanimous bliss, I am vast as space!

निर्भावभावरहितो न भवामि वत्स निर्योगयोगरहितो न भवामि वत्स ।
निश्चिन्तचिन्तरहितो न भवामि वत्स ज्ञानामृतं समरसं गगनोपमोऽहम् ॥ ११॥

nirbhava bhavarahito na bhavami vatsa niryoga yogarahito na bhavami vatsa |
nishchitta chittarahito na bhavami vatsa gnanamrutam samarasam gaganopamoham ||3-11||

I am free of existence and non-existence, these are not in me, child. I am free of union and separation, these are not in me, child. I am free of mindfulness and mindlessness, these are not in me, child. I am the nectar of knowledge, I am equanimous bliss, I am vast as space!

निर्मोहमोहपदवीति न मे विकल्पो निःशोकशोकपदवीति न मे विकल्पः ।
निर्लोभलोभपदवीति न मे विकल्पो ज्ञानामृतं समरसं गगनोपमोऽहम् ॥ १२॥

nirmoha moha padaviti na me vikalpah nihshoka shoka padaviti na me vikalpah |
nirlobha lobha padaviti na me vikalpah gnanamrutam samarasam gaganopamoham ||3-12||

I am free from illusion, I cannot even imagine the state of delusion. I am beyond grief, I cannot even imagine the state of grief. I am beyond greed, I cannot even imagine the state of greed. I am the nectar of knowledge, I am equanimous bliss, I am vast as space!

संसारसन्ततिलता न च मे कदाचित् सन्तोषसन्ततिसुखो न च मे कदाचित् ।
अज्ञानबन्धनमिदं न च मे कदाचित् ज्ञानामृतं समरसं गगनोपमोऽहम् ॥ १३॥

samsara santati lata na cha me kadachit santosa santati sukho na cha me kadachit |
agnana bandhanam idam na cha me kadachit gnanamrutam samaras am gaganopamoham ||3-13||

The vine of worldly existence does not affect me in the least. The entire expanse of contentment and pleasures does not affect me in the least. This bondage of ignorance does not affect me in the least. I am the nectar of knowledge, I am equanimous bliss, I am vast as space.

संसारसन्ततिरजो न च मे विकारः सन्तापसन्ततितमो न च मे विकारः ।
सत्त्वं स्वधर्मजनकं न च मे विकारो ज्ञानामृतं समरसं
गगनोपमोऽहम् ॥ १४॥

sansara santati rajo na cha me vikarah santapa santati tamo na cha me vikarah |
satvam svadharma janakam na cha me vikarah gnanamrutam samarasam gaganopamoham ||3-14||

The entire expanse of worldly passion (rajas) cannot cause any disturbance in me. The entire expanse of suffering caused by ignorance (tamas) cannot cause any disturbance in me. The entire expanse of righteousness generated by goodness (sattva) cannot cause any disturbance in me. I am the nectar of knowledge, I am equanimous bliss, I am vast as space.

सन्तापदुःखजनको न विधिः कदाचित् सन्तापयोगजनितं न मनः कदाचित् ।
यस्मादहङ्कृतिरियं न च मे कदाचित् ज्ञानामृतं समरसं
गगनोपमोऽहम् ॥ १५॥

santapa duhkha janako na vidhih kadachit santapa yoga janitam na manah kadachit |
yasmad ahankritir iyam na cha me kadachit gnanamrutam samarasam gaganopamoham ||3-15||

Suffering due to sorrow never arises in me in any manner whatsoever. Suffering due to the practice of yoga never arises in my mind. That from which ego is generated is never in me. I am the nectar of knowledge, I am equanimous bliss, I am vast as space.

निष्कम्पकम्पनिधनं न विकल्पकल्पं स्वप्नप्रबोधनिधनं न हिताहितं हि ।
निःसारसारनिधनं न चराचरं हि ज्ञानामृतं समरसं गगनोपमोऽहम् ॥ १६॥

nishkampa kampa nidhanam na vikalpa kalpam svapna Prabodha nidhanam na hitahitam hi |
nihsarasara nidhanam na characharam hi gnanamrutam samarasam gaganopamoham ||3-16||

Having destroyed both decisiveness and indecisiveness, I am neither doubtful nor firm. Having destroyed both dreaming and awakening, I do not see the advantage or disadvantage of either. Having destroyed both essence and essencelessness, I do not see the difference between animate and inanimate. I am the nectar of knowledge, I am equanimous bliss, I am vast as the sky!

नो वेद्यवेदकमिदं न च हेतुतर्क्यं वाचामगोचरमिदं न मनो न बुद्धिः ।
एवं कथं हि भवतः कथयामि तत्त्वं ज्ञानामृतं समरसं गगनोपमोऽहम् ॥ १७॥

no vedya vedakam idam na cha hetu tarkyam vacham agocharam idam na mano na buddhih |
evam katham hi bhavatah kathayami tattvam gnanamrutam samarasam gaganopamoham ||3-17||

I am neither the knower nor the known, nor the cause of knowledge. I am imperceptible through speech, mind or intellect. Indeed, how can I describe the ultimate Reality with words? I am the nectar of knowledge, I am equanimous bliss, I am vast as the sky.

निर्भिन्नभिन्नरहितं परमार्थतत्त्वमन्तर्बहिर्न हि कथं परमार्थतत्त्वम् ।
प्राक्सम्भवं न च रतं नहि वस्तु किञ्चित् ज्ञानामृतं समरसं
गगनोपमोऽहम् ॥ १८॥

nirbhinna bhinna rahitam paramartha tattvam antar bahirna hi katham paramartha tattvam |
prak sambhavam na cha ratam nahi vastu kinchit gnanamrutam samarasam gaganopamoham ||3-18||

I am beyond division and non-division, I am the supreme Reality. How can there be a within or without when I am the supreme Reality? I was there before existence but I am not attached to any object of existence. I am the nectar of knowledge, I am equanimous bliss, I am vast as the sky!

रागादिदोषरहितं त्वहमेव तत्त्वं दैवादिदोषरहितं त्वहमेव तत्त्वम् ।
संसारशोकरहितं त्वहमेव तत्त्वं ज्ञानामृतं समरसं गगनोपमोऽहम् ॥ १९॥

ragadi dosa rahitam tvaham eva tattvam daivadi dosha rahitam tvaham eva tattvam |
sansara shoka rahitam tvaham eva tattvam gnanamrutam samarasam gaganopamoham ||3-19||

Free from the faults of attachment, you and I are one Reality. Free from the faults of destiny, you and I are one Reality. Free from the sorrows of the worldly existence, you and I are one Reality. I am the nectar of knowledge, I am equanimous bliss, I am vast as the sky!

स्थानत्रयं यदि च नेति कथं तुरीयं कालत्रयं यदि च नेति कथं दिशश्च ।
शान्तं पदं हि परमं परमार्थतत्त्वं ज्ञानामृतं समरसं गगनोपमोऽहम् ॥ २०॥

sthana trayam yadi cha neti katham turiyam kala trayam yadi cha neti katham dishah cha |
shantam padam hi paramam paramartha tattvam gnanamrutam samarasam gaganopamoham ||3-20||

When I am not any of the three states of mind (waking, dreaming, deep sleep), how can I be the fourth state (pure awareness)? When I am not the three kinds of time (past, present, future), how can I be the fourth? I am the supreme foundation of serenity, I am the Absolute Reality. I am the nectar of knowledge, I am equanimous bliss, I am vast as the sky!

दीर्घो लघुः पुनरितीह नमे विभागो विस्तारसंकटमितीह न मे विभागः ।
कोणं हि वर्तुलमितीह न मे विभागो ज्ञानामृतं समरसं गगनोपमोऽहम् ॥ २१॥

dirgho laghuh punar itiha na me vibhagah vistara sankatam itiha na me vibhagah |
konam hi vartulam itiha na me vibhagah gnanamrutam samarasam gaganopamoham ||3-21||

Words like long or short cannot divide me (by defining me). Words like broad or narrow cannot divide me. Words like angular or round cannot divide me. I am the nectar of knowledge, I am equanimous bliss, I am vast as the sky!

मातापितादि तनयादि न मे कदाचित् जातं मृतं न च मनो न च मे कदाचित् ।
निर्व्याकुलं स्थिरमिदं परमार्थतत्त्वं ज्ञानामृतं समरसं गगनोपमोऽहम् ॥ २२॥

mata pitadi tanayadi na me kadachit jatam mrutam na cha mano ne cha me kadachit |
nirvyakulam sthiram idam paramartha tattvam gnanamrutam samarasam gaganopamoham ||3-22||

No mother, father or son was ever mine. No birth, death or mind was ever mine. I am untroubled and steady, I am the Absolute Reality. I am the nectar of knowledge, I am equanimous bliss, I am vast as the sky!

शुद्धं विशुद्धमविचारमनन्तरूपं निर्लेपलेपमविचारमनन्तरूपम् ।
निष्खण्डखण्डमविचारमनन्तरूपं ज्ञानामृतं समरसं गगनोपमोऽहम् ॥ २३॥

shuddham vishuddham avicharam anantarupam nirlepa lepam avicharam ananta rupam |
nishkhanda khandam avicharam ananta rupam gnanamrutam samarasam gaganopamoham ||3-23||

My nature is infinite, beyond concepts of purity or impurity. My nature is infinite, beyond concepts of stain or stainlessness. My nature is infinite, beyond thoughts of being broken or unbroken. I am the nectar of knowledge, I am equanimous bliss, I am vast as the sky!

ब्रह्मादयः सुरगणाः कथमत्र सन्ति स्वर्गादयो वसतयः कथमत्र सन्ति ।
यद्येकरूपममलं परमार्थतत्त्वं ज्ञानामृतं समरसं गगनोपमोऽहम् ॥ २४॥

brahmadayah sura ganah katham atra santi svargadayo vasatayah katham atra santi |
yadyekarupam amalam paramartha tattvam gnanamrutam samarasam gaganopamoham ||3-24||

How can Brahma and other gods be here, how can heaven and its residents be here, if I am the One, ultimate, stainless, supreme Reality? I am the nectar of knowledge, I am equanimous bliss, I am vast as the sky!

निर्नेति नेति विमलो हि कथं वदामि निःशेषशेषविमलो हि कथं वदामि ।
निर्लिङ्गलिङ्गविमलो हि कथं वदामि ज्ञानामृतं समरसं
गगनोपमोऽहम् ॥ २५॥

nirneti neti vimalo hi katham vadami nihshesha shesha vimalo hi katham vadami |
nirlinga linga vimalo hi katham vadami gnanamrutam samarasam gaganopamoham ||3-25||

How can I speak of that which is pure beyond both 'this' and 'not this'? How can I speak of that which is pure beyond being either complete or incomplete? How can I speak of that which is pure beyond gender definition or genderlessness? I am the nectar of knowledge, I am equanimous bliss, I am vast as the sky!

निष्कर्मकर्मपरमं सततं करोमि निःसङ्गसङ्गरहितं परमं विनोदम् ।
निर्देहदेहरहितं सततं विनोदं ज्ञानामृतं समरसं गगनोपमोऽहम् ॥ २६॥

nishkarma karma paramam satatam karomi nihsanga sanga rahitam paramam vinodam |
nirdeha deha rahitam satatam vinodam gnanamrutam samarasam gaganopamoham ||3-26||

I am always beyond both action and inaction. I am beyond attachment and non-attachment, always supremely blissful. I am beyond body and bodilessness, continuously blissful. I am the nectar of knowledge, I am equanimous bliss, I am vast as the sky!

मायाप्रपञ्चरचना न च मे विकारः । कौटिल्यदम्भरचना न च मे विकारः ।
सत्यानृतेति रचना न च मे विकारो ज्ञानामृतं समरसं
गगनोपमोऽहम् ॥ २७॥

maya prapancha rachana na cha me vikarah | kautilya dambha rachana na cha me vikarah |
satyanruteti rachana na cha me vikarah gnanamrutam samarasam gaganopamoham ||3-27||

This stage-play of maya does not cause any disturbance in me. The play of dishonesty or fraud does not cause any disturbance in me. The play of truth or falsehood does not cause any disturbance in me. I am the nectar of knowledge, I am equanimous bliss, I am vast as the sky!

सन्ध्यादिकालरहितं न च मे वियोगो-ह्यन्तः प्रबोधरहितं बधिरो न मूकः ।
एवं विकल्परहितं न च भावशुद्धं ज्ञानामृतं समरसं गगनोपमोऽहम् ॥ २८॥

sandhyadi kalarahitam na cha me viyogah hyantah prabodha rahitam badhiro na mukah |
evam vikalpa rahitam na cha bhava shuddham gnanamrutam samarasam gaganopamoham ||3-28||

Distinctions of time like evening etc. cannot cause a split in me. Manifesting or unmanifesting cannot make me deaf or mute. I am not pure "being", in fact, I am beyond all conceptualization. I am the nectar of knowledge, I am equanimous bliss, I am vast as the sky!

निर्नाथनाथरहितं हि निराकुलं वै निश्चिन्तचित्तविगतं हि निराकुलं वै ।
संविद्धि सर्वविगतं हि निराकुलं वै ज्ञानामृतं समरसं गगनोपमोऽहम् ॥ २९॥

nirnatha natha rahitam hi nirakulam vai nischitta chitta vigatam hi nirakulam vai |
samviddhi sarva vigatam hi nirakulam vai gnanamrutam samarasam gaganopamoham ||3-29||

Beyond being with or without God, I am undisturbed. Beyond being mindful or mindless, I am undisturbed. Know I am beyond everything, I am truly undisturbed. I am the nectar of knowledge, I am equanimous bliss, I am vast as the sky!

कान्तारमन्दिरमिदं हि कथं वदामि संसिद्धसंशयमिदं हि कथं वदामि ।
एवं निरन्तरसमं हि निराकुलं वै ज्ञानामृतं समरसं गगनोपमोऽहम् ॥ ३०॥

kantara mandiram idam hi katham vadami sansiddha sanshayam idam hi katham vadami |
evam nirantara samam hi nirakulam vai gnanamrutam samarasam gaganopamoham ||3-30||

How can I say whether this is wilderness or a temple? How can I say whether this is accomplishment or doubt? I am ceaselessly equanimous, untroubled! I am the nectar of knowledge, I am equanimous bliss, I am vast as the sky!

निर्जीवजीवरहितं सततं विभाति निर्बीजबीजरहितं सततं विभाति ।
निर्वाणबन्धरहितं सततं विभाति ज्ञानामृतं समरसं गगनोपमोऽहम् ॥ ३१॥

nirjiva jiva rahitam satatam vibhati nirbija bija rahitam satatam vibhati |
nirvana bandha rahitam satatam vibhati gnanamrutam samarasam gaganopamoham ||3-31||

Beyond being alive or lifeless, I ceaselessly shine forth. Beyond being potent or impotent, I ceaselessly shine forth. Beyond being liberated or bound, I ceaselessly shine forth. I am the nectar of knowledge, I am equanimous bliss, I am vast as the sky!

सम्भूतिवर्जितमिदं सततं विभाति संसारवर्जितमिदं सततं विभाति ।
संहारवर्जितमिअदं सततं विभाति ज्ञानामृतं समरसं गगनोपमोऽहम् ॥ ३२॥

sambhuti varjitam idam satatam vibhati sansara varjitam idam satatam vibhati |
samhara varjitam idam satatam vibhati gnanamrutam samarasam gaganopamoham ||3-32||

I am beyond a beginning, I ceaselessly shine forth. I am beyond this continuing world, I ceaselessly shine forth. I am beyond destruction, I ceaselessly shine forth. I am the nectar of knowledge, I am equanimous bliss, I am vast as the sky!

उल्लेखमात्रमपि ते न च नामरूपं निर्भिन्नभिन्नमपि ते न हि वस्तु किञ्चित् ।
निर्लज्जमानस करोषि कथं विषादं ज्ञानामृतं समरसं गगनोपमोऽहम् ॥ ३३॥

ullekhamatram api te na cha namarupam nirbhinna bhinnam api te na hi vastu kinchit |
nirlajja manasa karoshi katham vishadam gnanamrutam samarasam gaganopamoham ||3-33||

Even if you are spoken of, you have no name or form. Whether you are divided or undivided, you are not an object. O shameless mind, how can you lament so? I am the nectar of knowledge, I am equanimous bliss, I am vast as the sky!

किं नाम रोदिषि सखे न जरा न मृत्युः किं नाम रोदिषि सखे न च जन्म दुःखम् ।
किं नाम रोदिषि सखे न च ते विकारो ज्ञानामृतं समरसं गगनोपमोऽहम् ॥ ३४॥

kim nama rodishi sakhe na jara na murtyuh kim nama rodishi sakhe na cha janma duhkham |
kim nama rodishi sakhe na cha te vikarah gnanamrutam samarasam gaganopamoham ||3-34||

For what named object do you weep, my friend? There is no old age or death for you. For what named object do you weep, my friend? There is no pain of birth for you. For what named object do you weep, my friend? You have no disturbance in you. Realize – "I am the nectar of knowledge, I am equanimous bliss, I am vast as the sky!"

किं नाम रोदिषि सखे न च ते स्वरूपं किं नाम रोदिषि सखे न च ते विरूपम् ।
किं नाम रोदिषि सखे न च ते वयांसि ज्ञानामृतं समरसं गगनोपमोऽहम् ॥ ३५॥

kim nama rodishi sakhe na cha te svarupam kim nama rodishi sakhe na cha te virupam |
kim nama rodishi sakhe na cha te vayamsi gnanamrutam samarasam gaganopamoham ||3-35||

For what named object do you weep, my friend? You have no form of your own. For what named object do you weep, my friend? You have no deformity. For what named object do you weep, my friend? You are not subject to aging. Realize – "I am the nectar of knowledge, I am equanimous bliss, I am vast as the sky!"

किं नाम रोदिषि सखे न च ते वयांसि किं नाम रोदिषि सखे न च ते मनांसि ।
किं नाम रोदिषि सखे न तवेन्द्रियाणि ज्ञानामृतं समरसं गगनोपमोऽहम् ॥ ३६॥

kim nama rodishi sakhe na cha te vayamsi kim nama rodishi sakhe na cha te manamsi |
kim nama rodishi sakhe na tavendriyani gnanamrutam samarasam gaganopamoham ||3-36||

For what named object do you weep, my friend? You are not subject to aging. For what named object do you weep, my friend? You can never lose your mind. For what named object do you weep, my friend? You have no sense organs. Realize – "I am the nectar of knowledge, I am equanimous bliss, I am vast as the sky!"

किं नाम रोदिषि सखे न च तेऽस्ति कामः किं नाम रोदिषि सखे न च ते प्रलोभः ।
किं नाम रोदिषि सखे न च ते विमोहो ज्ञानामृतं समरसं गगनोपमोऽहम् ॥ ३७॥

kim nama rodishi sakhe na cha te asti kamah kim nama rodishi sakhe na cha te pralobhah |
kim nama rodishi sakhe na cha te vimohah gnanamrutam samarasam gaganopamoham ||3-37||

For what named object do you weep, my friend? Lust is never in you. For what named object do you weep, my friend? Greed is never in you. For what named object do you weep, my friend? Infatuation is never in you. Realize – "I am the nectar of knowledge, I am equanimous bliss, I am vast as the sky!"

ऐश्वर्यमिच्छसि कथं न च ते धनानि ऐश्वर्यमिच्छसि कथं न च ते हि पत्नी ।
ऐश्वर्यमिच्छसि कथं न च ते ममेति ज्ञानामृतं समरसं गगनोपमोऽहम् ॥ ३८॥

aishvaryam icchasi katham na cha te dhanani aishvaryam icchasi katham na cha te hi patni |
aishvaryam icchasi katham na cha te mameti gnanamrutam samarasam gaganopamoham ||3-38||

For what can you desire wealth? You have no treasure (to add to). For what can you desire wealth? You have no wife (to support). For what can you desire wealth? You have no sense of 'mine'. Realize – "I am the nectar of knowledge, I am equanimous bliss, I am vast as the sky!"

लिङ्गप्रपञ्चजनुषी न च ते न मे च निर्लज्जमानसमिदं च विभाति भिन्नम् ।
निर्भेदभेदरहितं न च ते न मे च ज्ञानामृतं समरसं गगनोपमोऽहम् ॥ ३९॥

linga prapancha janushi na cha te na me cha nirlajja manasam idam cha vibhati bhinnam |
nirbheda bheda rahitam na cha te na me cha gnanamrutam samarasam gaganopamoham ||3-39||

This stage of human forms is neither mine nor yours, it is only the shameless mind that perceives different forms. You and I are free of division and non-division. Realize – "I am the nectar of knowledge, I am equanimous bliss, I am vast as the sky!"

नो वाणुमात्रमपि ते हि विरागरूपं नो वाणुमात्रमपि ते हि सरागरूपम् ।
नो वाणुमात्रमपि ते हि सकामरूपं ज्ञानामृतं समरसं गगनोपमोऽहम् ॥ ४०॥

no vanumatram api te hi viraga rupam no vanumatram api te hi saraga rupam |
no vanumatram api te hi sakama rupam gnanamrutam samarasam gaganopamoham ||3-40||

There is not even an atom's worth of dispassion in you, there is not even an atom's worth of passion in you. There is not even an atom's worth of lust in you. Realize – "I am the nectar of knowledge, I am equanimous bliss, I am vast as the sky!"

ध्याता न ते हि हृदये न च ते समाधिर्ध्यानं न ते हि हृदये न बहिः प्रदेशः ।
ध्येयं न चेति हृदये न हि वस्तु कालो ज्ञानामृतं समरसं गगनोपमोऽहम् ॥ ४१॥

dhyata na te hi hridaye na cha te samadhih dhyanam na te hi hridaye na bahih pradeshah |
dhyeyam na cheti hridaye na hi vastu kalo gnanamrutam samarasam gaganopamoham ||3-41||

There is no meditator in your heart, there is no state of Samadhi. There is no act of meditation in your heart, there is no outer world. There is nobody to worship in your heart, there is no object or time. Realize – "I am the nectar of knowledge, I am equanimous bliss, I am vast as the sky!"

यत्सारभूतमखिलं कथितं मया ते न त्वं न मे न महतो न गुरुर्न न शिष्यः ।
स्वच्छन्दरूपसहजं परमार्थतत्त्वं ज्ञानामृतं समरसं गगनोपमोऽहम् ॥ ४२॥

yat sarabhutam akhilam kathitam maya te na tvam na me na mahato na guruh na shishyah |
svacchanda rupa sahajam paramartha tattvam gnanamrutam samarasam gaganopamoham ||3-42||

I have told you that which is the essential truth of this entire existence. There is no you, no me, no great being, no guru, no disciple. I am that Absolute Reality whose nature is innately spontaneous. Realize – "I am the nectar of knowledge, I am equanimous bliss, I am vast as the sky!"

कथमिह परमार्थं तत्त्वमानन्दरूपं कथमिह परमार्थं नैवमानन्दरूपम् ।
कथमिह परमार्थं ज्ञानविज्ञानरूपं यदि परमहमेकं वर्तते व्योमरूपम् ॥ ४३॥

katham iha paramartham tattvam ananda rupam katham iha paramartham naivam ananda rupam |
katham iha paramartham gnana vignana rupam yadi param aham ekam vartate vyoma rupam ||3-43||

How can the supreme Reality be found in a blissful state? How can the supreme Reality be found in a non-blissful state? How can the supreme Reality be found in knowledge or realization, when I myself am the supreme One, vast as space!

दहनपवनहीनं विद्धि विज्ञानमेकमवनिजलविहीनं विद्धि विज्ञानरूपम् ।
समगमनविहीनं विद्धि विज्ञानमेकं गगनमिव विशालं विद्धि विज्ञानमेकम् ॥ ४४॥

dahana pavana hinam viddhi vijnanam ekam avani jala vihinam viddhi vignana rupam |

samagamana vihinam viddhi vignanam ekam gaganam iva vishalam viddhi vignanam ekam ||3-44||

Know that it is beyond fire and air, realize the One! Know that it is beyond earth and water, realize the One! Know that it is beyond all coming and going, realize the One! Know that it is vast as space, realize the One!

न शून्यरूपं न विशून्यरूपं न शुद्धरूपं न विशुद्धरूपम् ।
रूपं विरूपं न भवामि किञ्चित् स्वरूपरूपं परमार्थतत्त्वम् ॥ ४५॥

na shunya rupam na vishunya rupam na shuddha rupam na vishuddha rupam |
rupam virupam na bhavami kinchit svarupa rupam paramartha tattvam ||3-45||

My nature is neither partial nor complete nothingness. My nature is neither partial nor complete purity. My nature is neither beauty nor deformity – not even a little of all these exist in me. My only nature is the Self - Absolute Reality!

मुञ्च मुञ्च हि संसारं त्यागं मुञ्च हि सर्वथा ।
त्यागात्यागविषं शुद्धमगृतं सहजं ध्रुवम् ॥ ४६॥

muncha muncha hi samsaram tyagam muncha hi sarvatha |
tyagatyaga visham shuddham amrutam sahajam dhruvam ||3-46||

Set aside, renounce the world, then renounce all renunciation as well! Renunciation and non-renunciation both are poison. The only one pure nectar is that which is innately changeless!

iti shri dattatreya virachitayam avadhuta gitayam atma samvittyupadesha nama tritiyodhyayah ||

In this Song of the Avadhuta composed by Shri Dattatreya, this is the third chapter on the teaching of the wisdom of the Self.

Chapter 4

अथ चतुर्थोऽध्यायः ।
atha chaturtha adhyayah |
Fourth Adhyaya

नावाहनं नैव विसर्जनं वा पुष्पाणि पत्राणि कथं भवन्ति ।
ध्यानानि मन्त्राणि कथं भवन्ति समासमं चैव शिवार्चनं च ॥ १॥

navahanam naiva visarjanam va pushpani patrani katham bhavanti |
dhyanani mantrani katham bhavanti samasamam chaiva shivarchanam cha ||4-1||

What is the point of prostrations or various rites with flowers and leaves? What is the point of meditation or the chanting of mantras? The worshipper and Shiva are exactly the same!

न केवलं बन्धविबन्धमुक्तो न केवलं शुद्धविशुद्धमुक्तः ।
न केवलं योगवियोगमुक्तः स वै विमुक्तो गगनोपमोऽहम् ॥ २॥

na kevalam bandha vibandha mukto na kevalam shuddha vishuddha muktah |
na kevalam yoga viyoga muktah sa vai vimukto gaganopamoham ||4-2||

I am not only free of partial and complete bondage, I am not only free of partial and complete purity, I am not only free of union and separation, I am freedom itself, just like the sky!

सञ्जायते सर्वमिदं हि तथ्यं सञ्जायते सर्वमिदं वितथ्यम् ।
एवं विकल्पो मम नैव जातः स्वरूपनिर्वाणमनामयोऽहम् ॥ ३॥

sanjayate sarvam idam hi tathyam sanjayate sarvam idam vitathyam |
evam vikalpo mama naiva jatah svarupa nirvanam anamayoham ||4-3||

All this creation is real, some say. All this creation is not real, some say. Such concepts do not arise in me. I am free of illusion (maya), my nature is freedom itself!

न साञ्जनं चैव निरञ्जनं वा न चान्तरं वापि निरन्तरं वा ।
अन्तर्विभिन्नं न हि मे विभाति स्वरूपनिर्वाणमनामयोऽहम् ॥ ४॥

na sanjanam chaiva niranjanam va na cha antaram vapi nirantaram va |
antarvibhinnam na hi me vibhati svarupa nirvanam anamayoham ||4-4||

I am neither faulty nor faultless. I am neither with an end nor endless. I do not perceive divisions or subdivisions. I am free of maya, my nature is freedom itself!

अबोधबोधो मम नैव जातो बोधस्वरूपं मम नैव जातम् ।
निर्बोधबोधं च कथं वदामि स्वरूपनिर्वाणमनामयोऽहम् ॥ ५॥

abodha bodho mama naiva jato bodha svarupam mama naiva jatam |
nirbodha bodham cha katham vadami svarupa nirvanam anamayoham ||4-5||

Ignorance or intelligence do not arise in me, various forms of intelligence do not arise in me. How then, can I talk about knowing or not knowing? I am free of maya, my nature is freedom itself!

न धर्मयुक्तो न च पापयुक्तो न बन्धयुक्तो न च मोक्षयुक्तः ।
युक्तं त्वयुक्तं न च मे विभाति स्वरूपनिर्वाणमनामयोऽहम् ॥ ६॥

na dharma yuktah na cha papa yuktah na bandha yuktah na cha moksha yuktah |
yuktam tvayuktam na cha me vibhati svarupa nirvanam anamayoham ||4-6||

I am tied neither to righteousness, nor to sin. I am tied neither to bondage nor to freedom. I cannot even conceive being tied to this or that. I am free of maya, my nature is freedom itself!

परापरं वा न च मे कदाचित् मध्यस्थभावो हि न चारिमित्रम् ।
हिताहितं चापि कथं वदामि स्वरूपनिर्वाणमनामयोऽहम् ॥ ७॥

paraparam va na cha me kadachit madhyastha bhavo hi na charimitram |
hitahitam chapi katham vadami svarupa nirvanam anamayoham ||4-7||

I have no concept of superiority or non-superiority. I am always neutral, with no enemies or friends. How then, can I talk about good or evil? I am free of maya, my nature is freedom itself!

नोपासको नैवमुपास्यरूपं न चोपदेशो न च मे क्रिया च ।
संवित्स्वरूपं च कथं वदामि स्वरूपनिर्वाणमनामयोऽहम् ॥ ८॥

nopasako naivam upasyarupam na chopadesho na cha me kriya cha |
samvit svarupam cha katham vadami svarupa nirvanam anamayoham ||4-8||

I am neither the worshipper nor the object of worship. I have no teachings or rites. What then, can I say about my nature that is knowledge itself? I am free of maya, my nature is freedom itself!

नो व्यापकं व्याप्यमिहास्ति किञ्चित् न चालयं वापि निरालयं वा ।
अशून्यशून्यं च कथं वदामि स्वरूपनिर्वाणमनामयोऽहम् ॥ ९॥

na vyapakam vyapyam ihasti kinchit na chalayam vapi niralayam va |
ashunya shunyam cha katham vadami svarupa nirvanam anamayoham ||4-9||

There is nothing here that pervades or is pervaded. There is nothing that is destroyed or indestructible. How then, can I talk about the void or non-void? I am free of maya, my nature is freedom itself!

न ग्राहको ग्राह्यकमेव किञ्चित् न कारणं वा मम नैव कार्यम् ।
अचिन्त्यचिन्त्यं च कथं वदामि स्वरूपनिर्वाणमनामयोऽहम् ॥ १०॥

na grahako grahyakam eva kinchit na karanam va mama naiva karyam |
achintya chintyam cha katham vadami svarupa nirvanam anamayoham ||4-10||

I am neither the subject nor the object at any time. I am neither the cause, nor the effect. How then, can I speak about what can or cannot be contemplated? I am free of maya, my nature is freedom itself!

न भेदकं वापि न चैव भेद्यं न वेदकं वा मम नैव वेद्यम् ।
गतागतं तात कथं वदामि स्वरूपनिर्वाणमनामयोऽहम् ॥ ११॥

na bhedakam vapi na chaiva bhedyam na vedakam mama naiva vedyam |
gatagatam tata katham vadami svarupa nirvanam anamayoham ||4-11||

I am neither the one who differentiates, nor that which is differentiated. I am neither the knower, nor the known. How then, can I speak about that which comes and goes? I am free of maya, my nature is freedom itself! ||4-11||

न चास्ति देहो न च मे विदेहो बुद्दिर्मनो मे न हि चेन्द्रियाणि ।
रागो विरागश्च कथं वदामि स्वरूपनिर्वाणमनामयोऽहम् ॥ १२॥

na chasti deho na cha me videho buddhih mano me na hi chendriyani |
rago viragah cha katham vadami svarupa nirvanam anamayoham ||4-12||

I am not embodied, nor am I without body. I have no intellect, mind or senses. How then, can I speak about passion or dispassion? I am free of maya, my nature is freedom itself!

उल्लेखमात्रं न हि भिन्नमुच्चैरुल्लेखमात्रं न तिरोहितं वै ।
समासमं मित्र कथं वदामि स्वरूपनिर्वाणमनामयोऽहम् ॥ १३॥

ullekha matram na hi bhinnam ucchaih ullekha matram na tirohitam vai |
samasamam mitra katham vadami svarupa nirvanam anamayoham ||4-13||

I cannot conceive even an allusion to division. I cannot conceive even an allusion to what has vanished in me. How then, friend, can I speak about 'equality' or 'inequality'? I am free of maya, my nature is freedom itself!

जितेन्द्रियोऽहं त्वजितेन्द्रियो वा न संयमो मे नियमो न जातः ।
जयाजयौ मित्र कथं वदामि स्वरूपनिर्वाणमनामयोऽहम् ॥ १४॥

jitendriyoham tvajitendriyo va na samyamo me niyamo na jatah |
jayajayau mitra katham vadami svarupa nirvanam anamayoham ||4-14||

There is no victory over the senses for me or for you. There is neither discipline, nor rules, nor classifications. How then, friend, can I speak about victory or defeat? I am free of maya, my nature is freedom itself!

अमूर्तमूर्तिर्न च मे कदाचिदाद्यन्तमध्यं न च मे कदाचित् ।
बलाबलं मित्र कथं वदामि स्वरूपनिर्वाणमनामयोऽहम् ॥ १५॥

amurta murtih na cha me kadachit adyanta madhyam na cha me kadachit |
balabalam mitra katham vadami svarupa nirvana anamayoham ||4-15||

There is no form or formlessness for me, there is no beginning, middle or end for me. How then, friend, can I speak of childhood or old age? I am free of maya, my nature is freedom itself!

मृतामृतं वापि विषाविषं च सञ्जायते तात न मे कदाचित् ।
अशुद्धशुद्धं च कथं वदामि स्वरूपनिर्वाणमनागयोऽहम् ॥ १६॥

mrutamrutam vapi vishavisham cha sanjayate tata na me kadachit |
ashuddha shuddham cha katham vadami svarupa nirvanam anamayoham ||4-16||

Mortality or immortality, evil or good – these never arise in me, child. How then, can I speak of purity or impurity? I am free of maya, my nature is freedom itself!

स्वप्नः प्रबोधो न च योगमुद्रा नक्तं दिवा वापि न मे कदाचित् ।
अतुर्यतुर्यं च कथं वदामि स्वरूपनिर्वाणमनामयोऽहम् ॥ १७॥

svapnah prabodho na cha yoga mudra naktam diva vapi na me kadachit |
aturya turyam cha katham vadami svarupa nirvanam anamayoham ||4-17||

Dreaming, awakening, yogic meditative states, day or night – these are never in me. How then, can I speak of the four or other states of mind? I am free of maya, my nature is freedom itself!

संविद्धि मां सर्वविसर्वमुक्तं माया विमाया न च मे कदाचित् ।
सन्ध्यादिकं कर्म कथं वदामि स्वरूपनिर्वाणमनामयोऽहम् ॥ १८॥

samviddhi mam sarva visarva muktam maya vimaya na cha me kadachit |
sandhyadikam karma katham vadami svarupa nirvanam anamayoham ||4-18||

Know well that I am beyond everything and nothing, there is no maya or its absence in me. How then, can I talk about duties of evening etc. (duties of the three divisions of the day)? I am free of maya, my nature is freedom itself!

संविद्धि मां सर्वसमाधियुक्तं संविद्धि मां लक्ष्यविलक्ष्यमुक्तम् ।
योगं वियोगं च कथं वदामि स्वरूपनिर्वाणमनामयोऽहम् ॥ १९॥

samviddhi mam sarva samadhi yuktam samviddhi mam lakshya vilakshya muktam |
yogam viyogam cha katham vadami svarupa nirvanam anamayoham ||4-19||

Know well that I am established forever in the state of Samadhi, know well that I am forever beyond achievement and non-achievement. How then, can I talk about union or separation? I am free of maya, my nature is freedom itself!

मूर्खोऽपि नाहं न च पण्डितोऽहं मौनं विमौनं न च मे कदाचित् ।
तर्कं वितर्कं च कथं वदामि स्वरूपनिर्वाणमनामयोऽहम् ॥ २०॥

murkhopi naham na cha panditoham maunam vimaunam na cha me kadachit |

tarkam vitarkam cha katham vadami svarupa nirvanam anamayoham ||4-20||

I am neither a fool, nor a learned expert, there is no silence or non-silence in me ever. How then, can I talk about reasoning or non-reasoning? I am free of maya, my nature is freedom itself!

पिता च माता च कुलं न जातिर्जन्मादि मृत्युर्न च मे कदाचित् ।
स्नेहं विमोहं च कथं वदामि स्वरूपनिर्वाणमनामयोऽहम् ॥ २१॥

pita cha mata cha kulam na jatih janmadi murtyurna cha me kadachit |
sneham vimoham cha katham vadami svarupa nirvanam anamayoham ||4-21||

I have neither father nor mother nor family nor caste, neither birth nor death are ever in me. How then, can I talk about affection or non-affection? I am free of maya, my nature is freedom itself!

अस्तं गतो नैव सदोदितोऽहं तेजोवितेजो न च मे कदाचित् ।
सन्ध्यादिकं कर्म कथं वदामि स्वरूपनिर्वाणमनामयोऽहम् ॥ २२॥

astam gato naiva sadoditoham tejo vitejo na cha me kadachit |
sandhyadikam karma katham vadami svarupa nirvanam anamayoham ||4-22||

I never set, I am forever a rising sun, there is never presence or absence of light in me! How then, can I speak about the duties of evening etc. (duties of the three junctures of the day)? I am free of maya, my nature is freedom itself!

असंशयं विद्धि निराकुलं मां असंशयं विद्धि निरन्तरं माम् ।
असंशयं विद्धि निरञ्जनं मां स्वरूपनिर्वाणमनामयोऽहम् ॥ २३॥

asanshayam viddhi nirakulam mam asanshayam viddhi nirantaram mam |
asamshayam viddhi niranjanam mam svarupa nirvanam anamayoham ||4-23||

Know without doubt that I am never disturbed, know without doubt that I am endless! Know without doubt that I am ever stainless. I am free of maya, my nature is freedom itself!

ध्यानानि सर्वाणि परित्यजन्ति शुभाशुभं कर्म परित्यजन्ति ।
त्यागामृतं तात पिबन्ति धीराः स्वरूपनिर्वाणमनामयोऽहम् ॥ २४॥

dhyanani sarvani parityajanti shubhashubham karma parityajanti |
tyagamrutam tata pibanti dhirah svarupa nirvanam anamayoham ||4-24||

They renounce all meditation, they renounce all good and evil – O child, the wise drink only that nectar of renunciation. I am free of maya, my nature is freedom itself!

विन्दति विन्दति न हि न हि यत्र छन्दोलक्षणं न हि न हि तत्र ।
समरसमग्नो भावितपूतः प्रलपति तत्त्वं परमवधूतः ॥ २५॥

vindati vindati na hi na hi yatra chhando lakshanam na hi na hi tatra |
samarasa magno bhavita putah pralapati tattvam param avadhutah ||4-25||

Where there is no knowing even upon knowing, there are no scriptures or diverse knowledge. Deeply immersed in equanimity, purified and in the highest spiritual state, I, the Avadhuta, thus speak of the Absolute Reality!

iti shri dattatreya virachitayam avadhuta gitayam svami kartika samvade svatma samvittyupadeshe svarupa nirnaya nama chaturthodhyayah ||

In this Song of the Avadhuta composed by Shri Dattatreya, this is the fourth chapter on the teaching of the wisdom of the Self.

Chapter 5

अथ पञ्चमोऽध्यायः ।

atha panchama adhyayah |

Fifth Adhyaya

ॐ इति गदितं गगनसमं तत् न परापरसारविचार इति ।
अविलासविलासनिराकरणं कथमक्षरबिन्दुसमुच्चरणम् ॥ १॥

aum iti gaditam gagana samam tat na paraparasara vichara iti |
avilasa vilasa nirakaranam katham akshara bindu
samuccharanam ||5-1||

The sound of the syllable 'aum' is equally spread like the sky, there are no thought concepts of 'absolute' or 'relative' within it. When concepts of manifestation and non-manifestation are eradicated, what is the need for even a drop of this utterance?

इति तत्त्वमसिप्रभृतिश्रुतिभिः प्रतिपादितमात्मनि तत्त्वमसि ।
त्वमुपाधिविवर्जितसर्वसमं किमु रोदिषि मानसि सर्वसमम् ॥ २॥

iti tat tvam asi prabhruti shrutibhih pratipaditam atmani tattvam asi |
tvam upadhi vivarjita sarvasamam kim u rodishi manasi sarvasamam ||5-2||

"Thou art that" the scriptures have said from the very beginning, and the Self also proclaims "Thou art that". You are free of all limitations, and equanimous to everything. Why then, do you grieve in your heart? You are equanimous to everything.

अधऊर्ध्वविवर्जितसर्वसमं बहिरन्तरवर्जितसर्वसमम् ।
यदि चैकविवर्जितसर्वसमं किमु रोदिषि मानसि सर्वसमम् ॥ ३॥

atha urdhva vivarjita sarvasamam bahirantara varjita sarvasamam |
yadi chaika vivarjita sarvasamam kim u rodishi manasi sarvasamam ||5-3||

Free of terms such as prostrate or upright, you are equanimous to everything. Free of terms such as within and without, you are equanimous to everything. Free of terms such as many or one, you are equanimous to everything. Why then, do you grieve in your heart? You are equanimous to everything.

न हि कल्पितकल्पविचार इति न हि कारणकार्यविचार इति ।
पदसन्धिविवर्जितसर्वसमं किमु रोदिषि मानसि सर्वरागम् ॥ ४॥

nahi kalpita kalpa vichara iti na hi karana karya vichara iti |
pada sandhi vivarjita sarva samam kim u rodishi manasi sarva samam ||5-4||

There are no such things as concepts or conceptualization, there are no such things as causes or causation. Beyond all words and word-combinations, you are equanimous to everything. Why then, do you grieve in your heart? You are equanimous to everything.

न हि बोधविबोधसमाधिरिति न हि देशविदेशसमाधिरिति ।
न हि कालविकालसमाधिरिति किमु रोदिषि मानसि सर्वसमम् ॥ ५॥

nahi bodha vibodha samadhih iti na hi desha videsha samadhih iti |
nahi kala vikala samadhih iti kim u rodishi manasi sarvasamam ||5-5||

There are no concepts of knowledge or ignorance in the state of samadhi. There are no concepts of local or foreign in the state of samadhi. There are no concepts of transience or eternity in the state of samadhi. Why then, do you grieve in your heart? You are equanimous to everything.

न हि कुम्भनभो न हि कुम्भ इति न हि जीववपुर्न हि जीव इति ।
न हि कारणकार्यविभाग इति किमु रोदिषि मानसि सर्वसमम् ॥ ६॥

na hi kumbha nabho na hi kumbha iti na hi jivavapurna hi jiva iti |
na hi karana karya vibhaga iti kim u rodishi manasi sarva samam ||5-6||

There is no space in the jar, there is not even a jar! There is no body to hold the soul, there is not even a soul! There is no division of cause and effect. Why then, do you grieve in your heart? You are equanimous to everything.

इह सर्वनिरन्तरमोक्षपदं लघुदीर्घविचारविहीन इति ।
न हि वर्तुलकोणविभाग इति किमु रोदिषि मानसि सर्वसमम् ॥ ७॥

iha sarva nirantara mokshapadam laghu dirgha vichara vihina iti |
na hi vartula kona vibhaga iti kim u rodishi manasi sarvasamam ||5-7||

Here in the state of ever-endless liberation, there are no concepts such as small or big. There are no distinctions such as round or angled. Why then, do you grieve in your heart? You are equanimous to everything.

इह शून्यविशून्यविहीन इति इह शुद्धविशुद्धविहीन इति ।
इह सर्वविसर्वविहीन इति किमु रोदिषि मानसि सर्वसमम् ॥ ८॥

iha shunya vishunya vihina iti iha shuddha vishuddha vihina iti |
iha sarva visarva vihina iti kim u rodishi manasi sarvasamam ||5-8||

This state here is free of concepts such as emptiness and fullness, it is free of purity and impurity, it is free of everything and nothing. Why then, do you grieve in your heart? You are equanimous to everything.

न हि भिन्नविभिन्नविचार इति बहिरन्तरसन्धिविचार इति ।
अरिमित्रविवर्जितसर्वसमं किमु रोदिषि मानसि सर्वसमम् ॥ ९॥

nahi bhinna vibhinna vichara iti bahir antara sandhi vichara iti |
ari mitra vivarjita sarva samam kim u rodishi manasi sarva samam ||5-9||

There are no concepts such as differences or equality. There are no concepts such as within, without, or the merging of the two. You are ever-equanimous, beyond distinctions such as friend or enemy. Why then, do you grieve in your heart? You are equanimous to everything.

न हि शिष्यविशिष्यस्वरूपैति न चराचरभेदविचार इति ।
इह सर्वनिरन्तरमोक्षपदं किमु रोदिषि मानसि सर्वसमम् ॥ १०॥

na hi shishya vishishya svarupa iti na charachara bheda vichara iti |
iha sarva nirantara mokshapadam kim u rodishi manasi sarvasamam ||5-10||

There are no forms such as disciple or non-disciple, there are no distinct concepts such as animate or inanimate. There is only the ever-endless state of liberation here. Why then, do you grieve in your heart? You are equanimous to everything.

ननु रूपविरूपविहीन इति ननु भिन्नविभिन्नविहीन इति ।
ननु सर्गविसर्गविहीन इति किमु रोदिषि मानसि सर्वसमम् ॥ ११॥

nanu rupa virupa vihina iti nanu bhinna vibhinna vihina iti |
nanu sarga visarga vihina iti kim u rodishi manasi sarvasamam ||5-11||

Indeed, it is beyond form and formlessness. Indeed, it is beyond division and non-division. Indeed, it is beyond creation and non-creation. Why then, do you grieve in your heart? You are equanimous to everything.

न गुणागुणपाशनिबन्ध इति मृतजीवनकर्म करोमि कथम् ।
इति शुद्धनिरञ्जनसर्वसमं किमु रोदिषि मानसि सर्वसमम् ॥ १२॥

na gunaguna pasha nibandha iti mruta jivana karma karomi katham |
iti shuddha niranjana sarvasamam kim u rodishi manasi sarvasamam ||5-12||

Neither the gunas nor anything else can bind it. How then, can life, death or actions bind it? It is pure, stainless, equanimous. Why then, do you grieve in your heart? You are equanimous to everything.

इह भावविभावविहीन इति इह कामविकामविहीन इति ।
इह बोधतमं खलु मोक्षसमं किमु रोदिषि मानसि सर्वसमम् ॥ १३॥

iha bhava vibhava vihina iti iha kama vikama vihina iti |
iha bodhatamam khalu mokshasamam kim u rodishi manasi sarvasamam ||5-13||

There is neither existence nor non-existence here. There is neither desire nor desirelessness here. There is only pure consciousness and oneness with freedom here. Why then, do you grieve in your heart? You are equanimous to everything.

इह तत्त्वनिरन्तरतत्त्वमिति न हि सन्धिविसन्धिविहीन इति ।
यदि सर्वविवर्जितसर्वसमं किमु रोदिषि मानसि सर्वसमम् ॥ १४॥

iha tattva virantara tattvam iti na hi sandhi visandhi vihina iti |
yadi sarva vivarjita sarvasamam kim u rodishi manasi sarvasamam ||5-14||

There is no everlasting reality or unreality here, there is no union or separation here. When you are equanimous and beyond everything, why do you grieve in your heart? You are truly equanimous to everything.

आनेकेतकुटी पारंवारसमं इहसङ्गविसङ्गविहीनपरम् ।
इह बोधविबोधविहीनपरं किमु रोदिषि मानसि सर्वसमम् ॥ १५॥

aniketa kuti parivara samam iha sanga visanga vihina param |
iha bodha vibodha vihina param kim u rodishi manasi
sarvasamam ||5-15||

Reality is the same whether one is homeless or in a home with family. It is supreme, beyond attachment or detachment. It is supreme, beyond knowledge or ignorance. Why then, do you grieve in your heart? You are equanimous to everything.

अविकारविकारमसत्यमिति अविलक्षविलक्षमसत्यमिति ।
यदि केवलमात्मनि सत्यमिति किमु रोदिषि मानसि सर्वसमम् ॥ १६॥

avikara vikaram asatyam iti avilaksha vilaksham asatyam iti |
yadi kevalam atmani satyam iti kim u rodishi manasi
sarvasamam ||5-16||

Distortion or non-distortion, both are false. Purposefulness or purposelessness, both are false. When only the Self is the truth, why do you grieve in your heart? You are equanimous to everything.

इह सर्वसमं खलु जीव इति इह सर्वनिरन्तरजीव इति ।
इह केवलनिश्चलजीव इति किमु रोदिषि मानसि सर्वसमम् ॥ १७॥

iha sarvasamam khalu jiva iti iha sarva nirantara jiva iti |
iha kevala nishchala jiva iti kim u rodishi manasi
sarvasamam ||5-17||

Indeed, there is only one equanimous soul here. There is only one ever-eternal soul here. There is only one changeless soul here. Why then, do you grieve in your heart? You are equanimous to everything.

अविवेकविवेकमबोध इति अविकल्पविकल्पमबोध इति ।
यदि चैकनिरन्तरबोध इति किमु रोदिषि मानसि सर्वसमम् ॥ १८॥

aviveka vivekam abodha iti avikalpa vikalpam abodha iti |
yadi chaika nirantara bodha iti kim u rodishi manasi sarvasamam ||5-18||

Discrimination or non-discrimination, both are ignorance. Imagination or non-imagination, both are ignorance. When there is only one eternal consciousness here, why do you grieve in your heart? You are equanimous to everything.

न हि मोक्षपदं न हि बन्धपदं न हि पुण्यपदं न हि पापपदम् ।
न हि पूर्णपदं न हि रिक्तपदं किमु रोदिषि मानसि सर्वसमम् ॥ १९॥

na hi mokshapadam nahi bandhapadam na hi punyapadam nahi papapadam |
na hi purnapadam nahi riktapadam kim u rodishi manasi sarvasamam ||5-19||

There is no state of liberation, there is no state of bondage, there is no state of virtue, and no state of sin. There is no state of completeness, and no state of emptiness. Why then, do you grieve in your heart? You are equanimous to everything.

यदि वर्णविवर्णविहीनसमं यदि कारणकार्यविहीनसमम् ।
यदिभेदविभेदविहीनसमं किमु रोदिषि मानसि सर्वसमम् ॥ २०॥

yadi varna vivarna vihina samam yadi karana karya vihina samam |
yadi bheda vibheda vihina samam kim u rodishi manasi sarvasamam ||5-20||

When you are equanimous beyond caste and castelessness, when you are equanimous beyond cause and effect, when you are equanimous beyond division and non-division, why do you grieve in your heart? You are equanimous to everything.

इह सर्वनिरन्तरसर्वचिते इह केवलनिश्चलसर्वचिते ।
द्विपदादिविवर्जितसर्वचिते किमु रोदिषि मानसि सर्वसमम् ॥ २१॥

iha sarva nirantara sarvachite iha kevala nishchala sarvachite |
dvipadadi vivarjita sarva chite kim u rodishi manasi
sarvasamam ||5-21||

Everything is limitless, everything is pure consciousness here. There is only the never-changing one, everything is pure consciousness here. Beyond being human or otherwise, everything is pure consciousness. Why then, do you grieve in your heart? You are equanimous to everything.

अतिसर्वनिरन्तरसर्वगतं अतिनिर्मलनिश्चलसर्वगतम् ।
दिनरात्रिविवर्जितसर्वगतं किमु रोदिषि मानसि सर्वसमम् ॥ २२॥

ati sarva nirantara sarvagatam ati nirmala nishchala sarvagatam |
dinaratri vivarjita sarvagatam kim u rodishi manasi
sarvasamam ||5-22||

It is perfectly ever-eternal, all-pervading. It is complete, pure, unchanging, all-pervading. Beyond day or night, it is all-pervading. Why then, do you grieve in your heart? You are equanimous to everything.

न हि बन्धविबन्धसमागमनं न हि योगवियोगसमागमनम् ।
न हि तर्कवितर्कसमागमनं किमु रोदिषि मानसि सर्वसमम् ॥ २३॥

na hi bandha vibandha samagamanam na hi yoga viyoga samagamanam |
na hi tarka vitarka samagamanam kim u rodishi manasi sarvasamam ||5-23||

It is neither bound nor free, it is a unified whole. It is neither united nor separated, it is a unified whole. It is neither thought nor reasoning, it is a unified whole. Why then, do you grieve in your heart? You are equanimous to everything.

इह कालविकालनिराकरणं अणुमात्रकृशानुनिराकरणम् ।
न हि केवलसत्यनिराकरणं किमु रोदिषि मानसि सर्वसमम् ॥ २४॥

iha kala vikala nirakaranam anumatra krushanu nirakaranam |
na hi kevala satya nirakaranam kim u rodishi manasi sarvasamam ||5-24||

Here, time and timelessness do not exist. Even atoms and their particles do not exist. Only Absolute Reality never ceases to exist. Why then, do you grieve in your heart? You are equanimous to everything.

इह देहविदेहविहीन इति ननु ... हीनपरम् ।
अभिधानविधानविहीनपरं कि ...

iha deha videha vihina iti ... svapna sushupti ... param |
abhidhana vidhana vihina param kim u rodishi manasi sarvasamam ||5-25||

There is neither body nor bodilessness here. The supreme is beyond sleeping or dreaming. The supreme is beyond expression or enumeration. Why then, do you grieve in your heart? You are equanimous to everything.

गगनोपमशुद्धविशालसमं अतिसर्वविवर्जितसर्वसमम् ।
गतसारविसारविकारसमं किमु रोदिषि मानसि सर्वसमम् ॥ २६॥

gaganopama shuddha vishala samam api sarva vivarjita sarvasamam |
gata sara visara vikara samam kim u rodishi manasi sarvasamam ||5-26||

It is equanimous, pure, vast like space. It is equanimous, completely transcending everything. It is equanimous, beyond all conclusions, non-conclusions and distortions. Why then, do you grieve in your heart? You are equanimous to everything.

इह धर्मविधर्मविरागतरमिह वस्तुविवस्तुविरागतरम् ।
इह कामविकामविरागतरं किमु रोदिषि मानसि सर्वसमम् ॥ २७॥

iha dharma vidharma viraga taram iha vastu vivastu viraga taram |
iha kama vikama viraga taram kim u rodishi manasi sarvasamam ||5-27||

Here there is no passion for righteousness or non-righteousness. Here there is no passion for objects or non-objects. Here there is no passion for desire or desirelessness. Why then, do you grieve in your heart? You are equanimous to everything.

सुखदुःखविवर्जितसर्वसममिह शोकविशोकविहीनपरम् ।
गुरुशिष्यविवर्जिततत्त्वपरं किमु रोदिषि मानसि सर्वसमम् ॥ २८॥

sukha duhkha vivarjita sarvasamam iha shoka vishoka vihina param |
guru shishya vivarjita tattvaparam kim u rodishi manasi
sarvasamam ||5-28||

Here, there is equanimity beyond joy and sorrow. The supreme is beyond grief or non-grief. Supreme Reality is beyond guru or disciple. Why then, do you grieve in your heart? You are equanimous to everything.

न किलाङ्कुरसारविसार इति न चलाचलसाम्यविसाम्यमिति ।
अविचारविचारविहीनमिति किमु रोदिषि मानसि सर्वसमम् ॥ २९॥

na kilankura sara visara iti na chalachala samya visamyam iti |
avichara vichara vihinam iti kim u rodishi manasi
sarvasamam ||5-21||

It does not sprout out of purposefulness or purposelessness, animateness or inanimateness, equanimity or non-equanimity. It is beyond thought and thoughtlessness. Why then, do you grieve in your heart? You are equanimous to everything.

इह सारसमुच्चयसारमिति । कथितं निजभावविभेद इति ।
विषये करणत्वमसत्यमिति किमु रोदिषि मानसि सर्वसमम् ॥ ३०॥

iha sara samucchaya saram iti | kathitam nijabhava vibheda iti |
vishaye karanatvam asatyam iti kim u rodishi manasi
sarvasamam ||5-30||

This is the highest essence of all principles. How then, can there be division in its own self? Every object of perception is false. Why then, do you grieve in your heart? You are equanimous to everything.

बहुधा श्रुतयः प्रवदन्ति यतो वियदादिरिदं मृगतोयसमम् ।
यदि चैकनिरन्तरसर्वसमं किमु रोदिषि मानसि सर्वसमम् ॥ ३१॥

bahudha shrutayah pravadanti yato viyadadih idam mrugatoya samam |
yadi chaika nirantara sarvasamam kim u rodishi manasi sarvasamam ||5-31||

The scriptures have said in many ways – the world and heaven are like water in a mirage. When there is only one eternal Reality, why do you grieve in your heart? You are equanimous to everything.

विन्दति विन्दति न हि न हि यत्र छन्दोलक्षणं न हि न हि तत्र ।
समरसमग्नो भावितपूतः प्रलपति तत्त्वं परमवधूतः ॥ ३२॥

vindati vindati na hi na hi yatra chhando lakshanam na hi na hi tatra |
samarasa magno bhavita putah pralapati tattvam param avadhutah ||5-32||

Where there is no knowing even upon knowing, there are no scriptures or diverse knowledge. Deeply immersed in equanimity, purified and in the highest spiritual state, I, the Avadhuta, thus speak of the Absolute Reality!

iti shri dattatreya virachitayam avadhuta gitayam swami kartika samvade atmasamvitti upadeshe sama drishti kathanam nama panchamodhyayah ||

In this Song of the Avadhuta composed by Shri Dattatreya, this is the Fifth Chapter on the teaching of the wisdom of the Self.

Chapter 6

अथ षष्ठमोऽध्यायः ।
atha shashthama adhyayah |
Sixth Adhyaya

बहुधा श्रुतयः प्रवदन्ति वयं वियदादिरिदं मृगतोयसमग् ।
यदि चैकनिरन्तरसर्वाशेवमुपमेयमथोह्युपमा च कथग् ॥ १॥

bahudha shrutayah pravadanti vayam viyadadir idam mrugatoya samam |
yadi chaika nirantara sarva shivam upameyam atho hyupama cha katham ||6-1||

The scriptures have told us in many ways – the world and heaven are like water in a mirage. If there is only one limitless Shiva (Self) who is everything, then how can it be compared, and to what?

अविभक्तिविभक्तिविहीनपरं ननु कार्यविकार्यविहीनपरम् ।
यदि चैकनिरन्तरसर्वशिवं यजनं च कथं तपनं च कथम् ।। २।।

avibhakti vibhakti vihina param nanu karya vikarya vihina param |
yadi chaika nirantara sarvashivam yajanam cha katham tapanam cha katham ||6-2||

The Supreme is free of division or non-division, the Supreme is free of action or inaction. If there is only one limitless Shiva who is everything, what is the need for sacrificial fires or austerities? ||6-2||

मन एव निरन्तरसर्वगतं ह्यविशालविशालविहीनपरम् ।
मन एव निरन्तरसर्वशिवं मनसापि कथं वचसा च कथम् ।। ३।।

mana eva nirantara sarvagatam hyavishala vishala vihina param |
mana eva nirantara sarvashivam manasapi katham vachasa cha katham ||6-3||

The One mind is infinite and all-pervading. It is supreme, beyond vastness or smallness. The One mind is limitless Shiva. How then, can it be found in thought or speech?

दिनरात्रिविभेदनिराकरणमुदितानुदितस्य निराकरणम् ।
यदि चैकनिरन्तरसर्वशिवं रविचन्द्रमसौ ज्वलनश्च कथम् ।। ४।।

dina ratri vibheda nirakaranam uditan uditasya nirakaranam |
yadi chaika nirantara sarva shivam ravi chandram asau jvalanashcha katham ||6-4||

The difference between night and day does not exist. The difference between sunrise and sunset does not exist. When there is only one, infinite Shiva who is everything, how can it be the sun and the moon which are shining?

गतकामविकामविभेद इति गतचेष्टविचेष्टविभेद इति ।
यदि चैकनिरन्तरसर्वशिवं बहिरन्तरभिन्नमतिश्च कथम् ॥ ५॥

gata kama vikama vibheda iti gata cheshta vicheshta vibheda iti |
yadi chaika nirantara sarva shivam bahir antara bhinna matih cha katham ||6-5||

It has transcended both desire and desirelessness. It has transcended both craving and non-craving. When there is only one limitless Shiva who is everything, how can there be thoughts of divisions such as without or within?

यदि सारविसारविहीन इति यदि शून्यविशून्यविहीन इति ।
यदि चैकनिरन्तरसर्वशिवं प्रथमं च कथं चरमं च कथम् ॥ ६॥

yadi sara visara vihina iti yadi shunya vishunya vihina iti |
yadi chaika nirantara sarva shivam prathamam cha katham charamam cha katham ||6-6||

If it is beyond both conclusions and non-conclusions, if it is beyond both emptiness and fullness, if there is only one limitless Shiva who is everything, how can there be a 'first' or a 'last'?

यदिभेदविभेदनिराकरणं यदि वेदकवेद्यनिराकरणम् ।
यदि चैकनिरन्तरसर्वशिवं तृतीयं च कथं तुरीयं च कथम ॥ ७॥

yadi bheda vibheda nirakaranam yadi vedaka vedya nirakaranam |
yadi chaika nirantara sarva shivam tritayam cha katham turiyam cha katham ||6-7||

If division and non-division do not exist, if the knower and the known do not exist, if there is only one limitless Shiva, how can there be a 'third' (mental state) or a 'fourth' (mental state)?

गदिताविदितं न हि सत्यमिति विदिताविदितं नहि सत्यमिति ।
यदि चैकनिरन्तरसर्वशिवं विषयेन्द्रियबुद्धिमनांसि कथम् ॥ ८ ॥

gadita viditam na hi satyam iti vidita viditam na hi satyam iti |
yadi chaika nirantara sarva shivam vishayendriya buddhi manamsi katham ||6-8||

What can be understood by speech is not the truth. What cannot be understood by speech is also not the truth. When there is only one limitless Shiva who is everything, how can objects, senses, intellect or mind exist?

गगनं पवनो न हि सत्यमिति धरणी दहनो न हि सत्यमिति ।
यदि चैकनिरन्तरसर्वशिवं जलदश्च कथं सलिलं च कथम् ॥ ९ ॥

gaganam pavano na hi satyam iti dharana dahano na hi satyam iti |
yadi chaika nirantara sarva shivam jaladash cha katham salilam cha katham ||6-9||

Neither space nor air is the truth. Neither earth nor fire is the truth. When there is only one limitless Shiva who is everything, how can the ocean exist and how can water?

यदि कल्पितलोकनिराकरणं यदि कल्पितदेवनिराकरणम् ।
यदि चैकनिरन्तरसर्वशिवं गुणदोषविचारमतिश्च कथम् ॥ १० ॥

yadi kalpita loka nirakaranam yadi kalpita deva nirakaranam |

yadi chaika nirantara sarva shivam gunadosha vichara matih cha katham ||6-10||

When the concept of the world does not exist, when the concept of heaven does not exist, when there is only one limitless Shiva who is everything, how can there be concepts such as the 'gunas' and their faults?

मरणामरणं हि निराकरणं करणाकरणं हि निराकरणम् ।
यदि चैकनिरन्तरसर्वशिवं गमनागमनं हि कथं वदति ॥ ११॥

maranamaranam hi nirakaranam karanakaranam hi nirakaranam |
yadi chaika nirantara sarva shivam gamanagamanam hi katham vadati ||6-11||

Death or life do not exist. Cause or effect do not exist. When there is only one limitless Shiva who is everything, how can one speak of going or coming?

प्रकृतिः पुरुषो न हि भेद इति न हि कारणकार्यविभेद इति ।
यदि चैकनिरन्तरसर्वशिवं पुरुषापुरुषं च कथं वदति ॥ १२॥

prakrutih purusho na hi bheda iti na hi karana karya vibheda iti |
yadi chaika nirantara sarva shivam purushapurusham cha katham vadati ||6-12||

There is no difference between matter (Prakriti) and consciousness (Purusha). When there is only one limitless Shiva who is everything, how can one speak of Self or not-Self?

तृतीयं न हि दुःखसमागमनं न गुणाद्द्वितीयस्य समागमनम् ।
यदि चैकनिरन्तरसर्वशिवं स्थविरश्च युवा च शिशुश्च कथम् ॥ १३॥

trutiyam na hi duhkha samagamanam na gunad dvitiyasya samagamanam |
yadi chaika nirantara sarva shivam sthavirah cha yuva cha shishuh cha katham ||6-13||

There is no third 'guna' (rajas) which brings one to misery. There is no second 'guna' (tamas) which brings one to misery. When there is only one limitless Shiva who is everything, how can there be old age, youth or childhood?

ननु आश्रमवर्णविहीनपरं ननु कारणकर्तृविहीनपरम् ।
यदि चैकनिरन्तरसर्वशिवमविनष्टविनष्टमतिश्च कथम् ॥ १४॥

nanu ashrama varna vihina param nanu karana kartru vihina param |
yadi chaika nirantara sarva shivam avinashta vinashta matih cha katham ||6-14||

The supreme is beyond stages of life, the supreme is beyond cause and effect. When there is only one limitless Shiva who is everything, how can there be concepts such as perishable or imperishable?

ग्रसिताग्रसितं च वितथ्यमिति जनिताजनितं च वितथ्यमिति ।
यदि चैकनिरन्तरसर्वशिवमविनाशि विनाशि कथं हि भवेत् ॥ १५॥

grasitagrasitam cha vitathyam iti janitajanitam cha vitathyam iti |
yadi chaika nirantara sarva shivam avinashi vinashi katham hi bhavet ||6-15||

Both the destroyer and the destroyed are false concepts. Both the knowable and unknowable are false concepts. When there is only one limitless Shiva who is everything, how can the perishable or the imperishable exist?

पुरुषापुरुषस्य विनष्टमिति वनितावनितस्य विनष्टमिति ।
यदि चैकनिरन्तरसर्वशिवमविनोदविनोदमतिश्च कथम् ॥ १६॥

purushapurushasya vinashtam iti vanitavanitasya vinashtam iti |
yadi chaika nirantara sarva shivam avinoda vinoda matih cha katham ||6-16||

Concepts such as male or non-male are destroyed. Concepts such as female or non-female are destroyed. When there is only one limitless Shiva who is everything, how can amusement or boredom exist?

यदि मोहविषादविहीनपरो यदि संशयशोकविहीनपरः ।
यदि चैकनिरन्तरसर्वशिवमहमेति ममेति कथं च पुनः ॥ १७॥

yadi moha vishada vihinaparo yadi sanshaya shoka vihina parah |
yadi chaika nirantara sarva shivam aham eti mameti katham cha punah ||6-17||

When the Supreme is beyond infatuation and lamentation, when the Supreme is beyond doubt and sorrow, when there is only one limitless Shiva who is everything, what is this sense of "I" and "mine"?

ननु धर्मविधर्मविनाश इति ननु बन्धविबन्धविनाश इति ।
यदि चैकनिरन्तरसर्वशिवंमिहदुःखविदुःखमतिश्च कथम् ॥ १८॥

nanu dharma vidharma vinasha iti nanu bandha vibandha vinasha iti |
yadi chaika nirantara sarva shivam iha duhkha viduhkha matih cha katham ||6-18||

There is no righteousness or non-righteousness – these are destroyed. There is no bondage or liberation – these are destroyed. When there is only one limitless Shiva who is everything, how can there be concepts such as sorrow or happiness here?

न हि याज्ञिकयज्ञविभाग इति न हुताशनवस्तुविभाग इति ।
यदि चैकनिरन्तरसर्वशिवं वद कर्मफलानि भवन्ति कथम् ॥ १९॥

na hi yagnika yagna vibhaga iti na hutashana vastu vibhaga iti |
yadi chaika nirantara sarva shivam vada karma phalani bhavanti katham ||6-19||

There is no distinction between the performer of the sacrificial rite, and the sacrificial rite itself. There is no distinction between the object of the sacrifice or the sacrificial fire. When there is only one limitless Shiva who is everything, tell me how can rewards for one's actions exist? ||6-19||

ननु शोकविशोकविमुक्त इति ननु दर्पविदर्पविमुक्त इति ।
यदि चैकनिरन्तरसर्वशिवं ननु रागविरागमतिश्च कथम् ॥ २०॥

nanu shoka vishoka vimukta iti nanu darpa vidarpa vimukta iti |
yadi chaika nirantara sarva shivam nanu raga viraga matih cha katham ||6-20||

Indeed, it is free of joy and sorrow. Indeed, it is free of pride and humility. When there is only one limitless Shiva who is everything, indeed, how can there be concepts such as passion or dispassion?

न हि मोहविमोहविकार इति न हि लोभविलोभविकार इति ।
यदि चैकनिरन्तरसर्वशिवं ह्यविवेकविवेकमतिश्च कथम् ॥ २१॥

na hi moha vimoha vikara iti na hi lobha vilobha vikara iti |
yadi chaika nirantara sarva shivam hyavivekaviveka matih cha katham ||6-21||

There are no distortions such as delusion or non-delusion. There are no distortions such as greed or non-greed. When there is only one limitless Shiva who is everything, how can there be concepts such as discrimination or non-discrimination?

त्वमहं न हि हन्त कदाचिदपि कुलजातिविचारमसत्यमिति ।
अहमेव शिवः परमार्थ इति अभिवादनमत्र करोमि कथम् ॥ २२॥

tvam aham na hi hanta kadachid api kula jati vicharam asatyam iti |
aham eva shivah paramartha iti abhivadanam atra karomi katham ||6-22||

Indeed! You and I have never ever existed! Concepts such as caste or creed are false. I, myself, am Shiva, the supreme Reality! To whom here then, should I offer my devotion?

गुरुशिष्यपतिनारतिशीर्ण इति उपदेशविचारविशीर्ण इति ।
अहमेव शिवः परमार्थ इति अभिवादनमत्र करोमि कथम् ॥ २३॥

guru shishya vichara vishirna iti upadesha vichara vishirna iti |
aham eva shivah paramartha iti abhivadanam atra karomi
katham ||6-23||

Concepts of guru and disciple are shattered. Concepts of teachings are shattered. I, myself, am Shiva, the supreme Reality!
To whom here then, should I offer my devotion?

न हि कल्पितदेहविभाग इति न हि कल्पितलोकविभाग इति ।
अहमेव शिवः परमार्थ इति अभिवादनमत्र करोमि कथम् ॥ २४॥

na hi kalpita deha vibhaga iti na hi kalpita loka vibhaga iti |
aham eva shivah paramartha iti abhivadanam atra karomi
katham ||6-24||

There are no concepts of separate bodies. There are no concepts of separate worlds. I, myself, am Shiva, the supreme Reality! To whom here then, should I offer my devotion?

सरजो विरजो न कदाचिदपि ननु निर्मलनिश्चलशुद्ध इति ।
अहमेव शिवः परमार्थ इति अभिवादनमत्र करोमि कथम् ॥ २५॥

sarajo virajo na kadachid api nanu nirmala nishchala shuddha iti |
aham eva shivah paramartha iti abhivadanam atra karomi
katham ||6-25||

There is no such thing as clean or unclean. Indeed, there is no stainlessness, changelessness or purity. I, myself, am Shiva, the supreme Reality! To whom here then, should I offer my devotion?

न हि देहविदेहविकल्प इति अनृतं चरितं न हि सत्यमिति ।
अहमेव शिवः परमार्थ इति अभिवादनमत्र करोमि कथम् ॥ २६॥

na hi deha videha vikalpa iti anrutam charitam na hi satyam iti |
aham eva shivah paramartha iti abhivadanam atra karomi katham ||6-26||

There are no concepts of body or bodilessness. Uncertainty or certainty both are false. I, myself, am Shiva, the supreme Reality! To whom here then, should I offer my devotion?

विन्दति विन्दति न हि न हि यत्र छन्दोलक्षणं न हि न हि तत्र ।
सगरसमग्नो भावितपूतः प्रलपति तत्त्वं परमवधूतः ॥ २७॥

vindati vindati na hi na hi yatra chhando lakshanam na hi na hi tatra |
samarasa magno bhavita putah pralapati tattvam param avadhutah ||6-27||

Where there is no knowing even upon knowing, there are no scriptures or diverse knowledge. Deeply immersed in equanimity, purified and in the highest spiritual state, I, the Avadhuta, thus speak of the Absolute Reality!

iti shri dattatreya virachitayam avadhuta gitaya swami kartika samvade svatma samvitti upadeshe moksha nirnavo nama sasto dhvayah ||

In this Song of the Avadhuta composed by Shri Dattatreya, this is the sixth chapter on the teaching of the wisdom of the Self.

Chapter 7

अथ सप्तमोऽध्यायः ।
atha saptama adhyayah |
Seventh Adhyaya

रथ्याकर्पटविरचितकन्थः पुण्यापुण्यविवर्जितपन्थः ।
शून्यागारे तिष्ठति नग्नो शुद्धनिरञ्जनसमरसमग्नः ॥ १॥

rathya karpata virachita kanthah punyapunya vivarjita panthah |
shunyagare tishati nagno shuddha niranjana samarasa magnah ||7-1||

An old rag crushed beneath chariots may serve as the garment of the one who walks on the path beyond virtue and sin. He lives naked in an empty hut - pure, stainless, immersed in equanimity.

लक्ष्यालक्ष्यविवर्जितलक्ष्यो युक्तायुक्तविवर्जितदक्षः ।
केवलतत्त्वनिरञ्जनपूतो वादविवादः कथमवधूतः ॥ २॥

lakshyalakshya vivarjita lakshyo yuktayukta vivarjita dakshah |
kevala tattva niranjana putah vadavivadah katham
avadhutah ||7-2||

His goal is beyond aim and aimlessness. His wisdom is beyond sensibility and insensibility. He is established only in stainless and pure Reality. How then, can the Avadhuta get into speeches and discussions?

आशापाशविबन्धनमुक्ताः शौचाचारविवर्जितयुक्ताः ।
एवं सर्वविवर्जितशान्तस्तत्त्वं शुद्धनिरञ्जनवन्तः ॥ ३॥

ashapasha vibandhana muktah shauchachara vivarjita yuktah |
evam sarva vivarjita shantah tattvam shuddha
niranjanavantah ||7-3||

He is free of bondage from the rope of hope. He is free from the harness of acceptable conduct. Thus free from everything, he is pure and stainless - the very essence of peace.

कथमिह देहविदेहविचारः कथमिह रागविरागविचारः ।
निर्मलनिश्चलगगनाकारं स्वयमिह तत्त्वं सहजाकारम् ॥ ४॥

katham iha deha videha vicharah katham iha raga viraga vicharah |
nirmala nischala gaganakaram svayam iha tattvam
sahajakaram ||7-4||

Where is the thought of body or bodilessness? Where is the thought of passion or passionlessness? Pure and unchanging like the sky, he himself is truth in its natural form.

कथमिह तत्त्वं विन्दति यत्र रूपमरूपं कथमिह तत्र ।
गगनाकारः परमो यत्र विषयीकरणं कथमिह तत्र ॥ ५॥

katham iha tattvam vindati yatra rupam arupam katham iha tatra |
gaganakarah paramo yatra vishayi karanam katham iha
tatra ||7-5||

Where there is the Absolute Reality, how can there be knowledge or the presence or absence of forms? Where there is the Supreme, infinite as the sky, how can there be perception of sense objects?

गगनाकारनिरन्तरहंसस्तत्त्वविशुद्धनिरञ्जनहंसः ।
एवं कथमिह भिन्नविभिन्नं बन्धविबन्धविकारविभिन्नम् ॥ ६॥

gaganakara nirantara hansah tattva vishuddha niranjana hamsah |
evam katham iha bhinna vibhinnam bandha vibandha vikara
vibhinnam ||7-6||

The Self is infinite like the sky, the Self is pure, stainless Reality. How then, can there be division or non-division, bondage or liberation, distortions or divisions?

केवलतत्त्वनिरन्तरसर्वं योगवियोगौ कथमिह गर्वम् ।
एवं परमनिरन्तरसर्वमेवं कथमिह सारविसारम् ॥ ७॥

kevala tattva nirantara sarvam yoga viyogau katham iha garvam |
evam parama nirantara sarvam evam katham iha sara visaram ||7-7||

102

There is only one limitless Reality everywhere. Where then, is union or separation or pride here? That One is supreme, never-ending and everything there is! How can that Supreme One have substance or non-substance here?

केवलतत्त्वनिरञ्जनसर्वं गगनाकारनिरन्तरशुद्धम् ।
एवं कथमिह सङ्गविसङ्गं सत्यं कथमिह रङ्गविरङ्गम् ॥ ८॥

kevala tattva niranjana sarvam gaganakara nirantara shuddham |
evam katham iha sanga visangam satyam katham iha ranga virangam ||7-8||

Everything is only one stainless Reality. It is pure and limitless like the sky. How then, can it be together or separate? How can this truth be colourful or colourless?

योगवियोगैः रहितो योगी भोगविभोगैः रहितो भोगी ।
एवं चरति हि मन्दं मन्दं मनसा कल्पितसहजानन्दम् ॥ ९॥

yoga viyogai rahito yogi bhoga vibhogai rahito bhogi |
evam charati hi mandam mandam manasa kalpita sahaj anandam ||7-9||

He is a yogi who is beyond union or separation. He is an enjoyer who is beyond enjoyment or non-enjoyment. He walks slowly and leisurely, while his mind experiences natural bliss.

बोधविबोधैः सततं युक्तो द्वैताद्वैतैः कथमिह मुक्तः ।
सहजो विरजः कथमिह योगी शुद्धनिरञ्जनसमरसभोगी ॥ १०॥

bodha vibodhaih satatam yukto dvaitadvaitaih katham iha muktah |
sahajo virajah katham iha yogi shuddha niranjana samarasa
bhogi ||7-10||

How can the one who is constantly obsessed with knowledge and ignorance, duality and non-duality, be considered liberated? How can a yogi be considered simple or passion-free? Isn't he an avid enjoyer of One, pure, stainless equanimity?

भग्नाभग्नविवर्जितभग्नो लग्नालग्नविवर्जितलग्नः ।
एवं कथमिह सारविसारः समरसतत्त्वं गगनाकारः ॥ ११॥

bhagna abhagna vivarjita bhagno lagnalagna vivarjita lagnah |
evam katham iha sara visarah samarasa tattvam
gaganakarah ||7-11||

He is the divider who is beyond division and non-division. He is the unifier who is beyond union and separation. How then, can he who is equanimous and all-pervading like the sky, be subject to principles or non-principles here?

सततं सर्वविवर्जितयुक्तः सर्वं तत्त्वविवर्जितमुक्तः ।
एवं कथमिह जीवितमरणं ध्यानाध्यानैः कथमिह करणम् ॥ १२॥

satatam sarva vivarjita yuktah sarvam tattva vivarjita muktah |
evam katham iha jivita maranam dhyanadhyanaih katham iha
karanam ||7-12||

He is constantly one with, yet beyond everything! He is one Reality, beyond everything, and free. How can there be life or death for him? How can there be meditation or non-meditation for him?

इन्द्रजालमिदं सर्वं यथा मरुमरीचिका ।
अखण्डितमनाकारो वर्तते केवलः शिवः ॥ १३॥

indrajalam idam sarvam yatha maru marichika |
akhanditam anakara vartate kevalah shivah ||7-13||

All this everywhere is a web of illusion, like the water of a mirage. Reality is only Shiva, unbroken, formless.

धर्मादौ मोक्षपर्यन्तं निरीहाः सर्वथा वयम् ।
कथं रागविरागैश्च कल्पयन्ति विपश्चितः ॥ १४॥

dharmadau moksha paryantam nirihah sarvatha vayam |
katham raga viragaish cha kalpayanti vipashchitah ||7-14||

We are transcendental to righteousness and liberation, indifferent to everything! How then, could we wise ones ever even imagine passion or passionlessness?

विन्दति विन्दति न हि न हि यत्र छन्दोलक्षणं न हि न हि तत्र ।
समरसमग्नो भावितपूतः प्रलपति तत्त्वं परमवधूतः ॥ १५॥

vindati vindati na hi na hi yatra chhando lakshanam na hi na hi tatra |
samarasa magno bhavita putah pralapati tattvam param avadhutah ||7-15||

Where there is no knowing even upon knowing, there are no scriptures or diverse knowledge. Deeply immersed in equanimity, purified and in the highest spiritual state, I, the Avadhuta, thus speak of the Absolute Reality!

iti shri dattatreyavirachitayam avadhuta gitayam swami kartika samvade svatma samvitti upadeshe saptamo adhyayah ||

In this Song of the Avadhuta composed by Shri Dattatreya, this is the seventh chapter on the teaching of the wisdom of the Self.

Chapter 8

अथ अष्टमोऽध्यायः ।

atha ashtama adhyayah |

Eighth Adhyaya

त्वद्यात्रया व्यापकता हता ते ध्यानेन चेतःपरता हता ते ।
स्तुत्या मया वाक्परता हता ते क्षमस्व नित्यं त्रिविधापराधान् ॥ १॥

tvad yatraya vyapakata hata te dhyanena chetah parata hata te |
stutya maya vakparata hata te kshamasva nityam trividha paradhan ||8-1||

In my journey towards you, your all-pervasiveness has been destroyed! Through my meditation, the sense of the superiority of your consciousness has been destroyed! By singing hymns unto you, the sense of your superiority of speech has been destroyed! Please always forgive these threefold tendencies in me.

कामैरहतधीर्दान्तो मृदुः शुचिरकिञ्चनः ।
अनीहो मितभुक् शान्तः स्थिरो मच्छरणो मुनिः ॥ २॥

kamai rahat adhirdanto mruduh shuchih akinchanah |
aniho mitabhuk shantah sthiro machharano munih ||8-2||

Free of lust, wise, restrained, gentle, always pure, indifferent, calm, steady, and with all hungers vanished, is the sage who has taken refuge in me.

अप्रमत्तो गभीरात्मा धृतिमान् जितषड्गुणः ।
अमानी मानदः कल्पो मैत्रः कारुणिकः कविः ॥ ३॥

apramatto gabhiratma dhrutiman jitashadgunah |
amani manadah kalpo maitrah karunikah kavih ||8-3||

The profoundly wise soul is deeply intelligent and aware, has triumphed over the six 'gunas' (five senses and the mind), is not arrogant but respectful to others, is deeply insightful, friendly and compassionate towards all.

कृपालुरकृतद्रोहस्तितिक्षुः सर्वदेहिनाम् ।
सत्यसारोऽनवद्यात्मा समः सर्वोपकारकः ॥ ४॥

krupaluh akrutadrohah titikshuh sarvadehinam |
satyasara anavadya atma samah sarva upakarakah ||8-4||

He is merciful, non-violent, compassionate and soft towards all embodied beings. He is the essence of truth, an innocent soul, equanimous and the benefactor of all.

अवधूतलक्षणं वर्णैर्ज्ञातव्यं भगवत्तमैः ।
वेदवर्णार्थतत्त्वज्ञैर्वेदवेदान्तवादिभिः ॥ ५॥

avadhuta lakshanam varneh gnatavyam bhagavattamaih |
vedavarna arthatattvagnaih vedavedantavadibhih ||8-5||

The qualities of the Avadhuta and the meaning of the syllables are known by the blessed ones who know the meaning of the syllables of the Vedas and their essence, who know and talk about the Vedas and Vedanta.

आशापाशविनिर्मुक्त आदिमध्यान्तनिर्मलः ।
आनन्दे वर्तते नित्यमकारं तस्य लक्षणम् ॥ ६॥

ashapashavinirmukta adim adhyanta nirmalah |
anande vartate nityam akaram tasya lakshanam ||8-6||

The quality pertaining to the sound 'A' in 'Avadhuta' is – one who is free from the bondage of hope (asha pasha vinirmukta), who is free of beginning, middle and end (adimadhyanta nirmala), and who always stays in the state of happiness (ananda).

वासना वर्जिता येन वक्तव्यं च निरामयम् ।
वर्तमानेषु वर्तेत वकारं तस्य लक्षणम् ॥ ७॥

vasana varjita yena vaktavyam cha niramayam |
vartamaneshu varteta vakaram tasya lakshanam ||8-7||

The quality pertaining to the sound 'va' in 'Avadhuta' is – one who is free of lust (vasana varjita), whose speech (vaktavya) is free of negativity, and who always stays in the present (vartamana).

धूलिधूसरगात्राणि धूतचित्तो निरामयः ।
धारणाध्याननिर्मुक्तो धूकारस्तस्य लक्षणम् ॥ ८॥

dhulidhusaragatrani dhutachitto niramayah |
dharanadhyana nirmukto dhukarastasya lakshanam ||8-8||

The quality pertaining to the sound 'dha' in 'Avadhuta' is – one whose limbs are covered in dust (dhulidha), whose mind is devoid of all negativity (dhutachitta), and who is free from all efforts towards concentration and meditation (dharana, dhyana).

तत्त्वचिन्ता धृता येन चिन्ताचेष्टाविवर्जितः ।
तमोऽहंकारनिर्मुक्तस्तकारस्तस्य लक्षणम् ॥ ९॥

tattvachinta dhruta yena chintacheshta vivarjitah |
tamo ahankara nirmuktasta karastasya lakshanam ||8-9||

The quality pertaining to the sound 'ta' in 'Avadhuta' is – one who deeply contemplates on the truth (tattvachinta dhruta), who is free of worries and desires (chinta, cheshta), and who is free of ignorance and ego (tamoahankara).

दत्तात्रेयावधूतेन निर्मितानन्दरूपिणा ।
ये पठन्ति च शृण्वन्ति तेषां नैव पुनर्भवः ॥ १०॥

dattatreya avadhutena nirmita anandarupina |
ye pathanti cha shrunvanti tesham naiva punarbhavah ||8-10||

This song of the Avadhuta has been composed in joy by Dattatreya. Whoever reads this or hears this never has to undergo rebirth.

In this Song of the Avadhuta composed by Shri Dattatreya, this is the eighth chapter on the teaching of the wisdom of the Self.

The End.

ॐ

Printed in Great Britain
by Amazon